Endangered Mammals of India

Dr. C. Veerabahu
Associate Professor
P.G. Department of Zoology and Research Centre
V.O.Chidambaram College,
Thoothukudi, Tamilnadu

Dr. D. Radhika
Reader
P.G. Department of Zoology and Research Centre
V.O.Chidambaram College,
Thoothukudi, Tamilnadu

ibdc publishers
PUBLISHING GREEN

Published by

ibdc publishers
PUBLISHING GREEN

Khushnuma Complex, Basement,
7, Meerabai Marg,
(Behind Jawahar Bhawan),
Lucknow - 226 001, U.P., India
Tel. : +91-522-2209542/ 42/ 44/ 45
Fax : +91-522-4045308
E-mail : ibdco@airtelmail.in
Website : www.ibdco.co.in

First Edition 2010

ISBN 978-81- 8189-490-8

Composed & Designed at :
Panacea Computers
3rd Floor, Agrawal Sabha Bhawan
Subhash Mohal, Sadar Cantt. Lucknow-226 002
Phone : 0522-2483312, 9335927082, 9452295008
E-mail : prasgupt@rediffmail.com

Printed at:
Salasar Imaging Systems
C-7/5, Lawrence Road Industrial Area
Delhi - 110 035
Tel. : 011-27185653, 9810064311

Dedicated to
the Guardian of our heart and
the Soul of our moral being,
Our beloved Bhagawan
Sri Sri Sri Sathya Sai Baba Varu

Dr. R. ANNAMALAI, I.F.S.,
Director

DEPARTMENT OF ENVIRONMENT,
Ground Floor, Panagai Building
No.1 Jeenis Road, Saldapet,
Chennai - 600 015

FOREWORD

I have gone through the book "Endangered Mammals of India" authored by Dr. C. Veerabahu & Dr. D. Radhika. I am impressed by the scholarly presentation of the endangered animals of our country, well detailed and documented. I am sure that this book will be of immense value not only to the students of Zoology and research Scholars in this particular field, but also to the general seekers of knowledge interested in the Fauna of our country. Details of taxonomic classificationand vital statistics regarding each species have been well presented. The book thus offers a wealth of knowledge even to a casual reader. I hope that this book will be much sought after by the learners in this field and I am certain it will find its worthy place in the Libraries of the institutions of higher learning.

18/11/2008

Dr. R. Annamali, I.F.S.
Director
Department of Environment
Chennai, Tamil Nadu

PREFACE

India can boast on its infinite variety of wild animals and birds. Out of 4629 species of mammals in the world, nearly 390 species exist in India. So it is the duty of every Indian to protect these wild animals from extinction. In 1940's for example, there were about 40,000 cheetahs found in India, but none is alive today.

In 2006, CITES- The Convention on wild International Trade in Endangered Species of fauna and flora has estimated about 5624 species of wild animals that are on the verge of extinction. According to IUCN, International union for conservation of Nature and Natural Resources 172 species of wild animals in India are on the verge of extinction, of which 53 are species of mammals, 23 are species of reptiles, 69 are species of aves and 3 are species of amphibians.

There are many books available with reference to the wild animals in the world. But there is no book that comprehensively deals with the wild animals in India especially the endangered ones. The authors have well attempted to focus on to these endangered species. The list of the endangered species in the book is a revelation to us. An urgent step by the Government is essential now to save these endangered animals from becoming extinct.

The book wakes up the readers to the shocking reality that most of the animals which are native to India are fast becoming extinct. This book will certainly be of immense use to the students of schools, colleges and Researchers in this field. Also it will create awareness among them about the diminishing wild life in the world, especially in India.

Authors

Alma mater of the Authors

V.O.Chidambaram College named after great patriot & freedom fighter, Swadeshi Navigator Cekkilutha Cemmal Late V.O.Chidambaram Pillai was founded in Tuticorin by my grand father Kulapathi A.P.C.Veerabahu in the year 1951. The eminent scholar Prof. A. Srinivasa Raghavan, Principal of the college joined hands with founder secretary and nurtured this college into a temple of learning, mainly catering to the needs of the poor and down trodden sections of the society of this part of South Tamilnadu .

College is offering 11 under graduate degree courses, 8 post graduate degree courses and 5 M.Phil. Programmes. PG Departments of Zoology, Chemistry, Geology, Mathematics and Botany have been recognized as research centres, where scholars pursue their research work leading to the award of Ph.D. degree. The college is co-educational and stands for the great ideals of Nationalism and Secularism. This college is one of the biggest affiliated colleges of Manonmaniam Sundaranar University, Tirunelveli.

This institution is Government aided and accredited by National Assessment and Accreditation Council (NAAC) with 'A' Grade in 2004.

The authors have the opportunity of serving this great institution of higher learning.

Contents

VULNERABLE

LEAST CONCERN

Wild Life

India's major natural resources are forests, wet lands, mangroves and wild life. The term wild life commonly represents the undomesticated animals living in their natural habitat. But in its widest sense it includes all the flora and fauna of the country. It is endowed with a particularly rich biological heritage, and the scriptures and epics of the nation have a distinct accounts of the wild life.

It is a great natural resource comprising 12, 63, 186 (IUCN - 2007) species of animals living in the world. Out of them, 1, 30, 000 (www.wildlife-tour-india.com) animals excist in India starting from protozoa to mammals which include 2546 species of fishes, 197 species of amphibians, more than 408 species of reptiles, 1250 species of birds, 410 species of mammals and innumerable species of insects and other vertebrates. (IUCN - 2006)

IUCN (International Union for Conservation of Natural & Natural Resources) has classified some animals in their Red Data book considered as endangered species. That is given as follows based on the history of distribution, decline in number of individuals, nature of habitat and the potential value of species;

1. Extinct (EX)
2. Extinct in the wild (EW)
3. Critically Endangered (CR)
4. Endangered (EN)
5. Vulnerable (VU)
6. Near threatened (NT)
7. Least Concern (LC)

Extinct: The last remaining member of the species has died (or) is presumed beyond doubt to have died.

Example: Dinosaurs

Extinct in the Wild: Captive individuals survive, but there is none free-living in the natural population.

Example: Indian cheetah.

Critically Endangered: The animal face an extremely high risk of extinction in the immediate future.

Example: Pygmy Hog, Jenkin's Shrew, Wroghton's free tailed Bat etc.

Endangered: They face a very high risk of extinction in the near future.

Example: Asiatic Lion, Tiger, Snow Leopard, Red Panda etc.

Vulnerable: They face a high risk of extinction in the medium-term.

Example: Black buck, Brown Bear, Banteng, Gaur etc.

Near Threatened: They may be considered as threatened in the near future.

Example: Solitary Eagle, Maned wolf, Small Clawed otter etc.

Least Concern; In this category no immediate threat to the survival of the species.

Example: Leopard, Red fox etc.

Hence, steps have been taken to protect and manage the endangered species of flora and fauna of the country.

So India can be proud of its rich bio-diversity which includes the variety of wild animals and birds. Many species of animals, native to India, are fast becoming extinct. According to IUCN, International union for conservation of Nature and Natural Resources 172 species of wild animals in India are on the verge of extinction, of which 53 are species of mammals, 23 are species of reptiles, 69 are species of aves and 3 are species of amphibians are on the verge of being threatened. Unless, these endangered animals are protected and saved from extinction, the country will not be able to maintain the balance in nature among the various species of animals (Both herbivores and carnivores). Why do we protect and conserve the wild animals? Why are the wild animals facing danger of extinction? What is the reason behind it?

The basic reasons of extinction of wildlife are as follows,

1. Destruction of their forest (or) natural habitats due to expanding agriculture, urbanization and industrialization.
2. Overgrazing by domestic animals that convert the area into deserts.
3. Poaching for meat, skin, fur, ivory etc.

If the wildlife scenario persists, there will be no flora and fauna left in the country. It will see them only in pictures.

The departments of Forestry & wildlife have been primarily under control of Government of India. However, quite recently the subject

Bio-geographic Zones

India is divided into ten bio-geographic zones, for example, the Himalaya and the Deccan, based on a distinctive set of physical and historical conditions. These are further divided into 23 biotic provinces, such as the North-western Himalaya and Chhota Nagpur Plateau. The major ecosystem groupings that are found in each of the biotic provinces are called biomes, for example, coastal, alpine, and scrub.

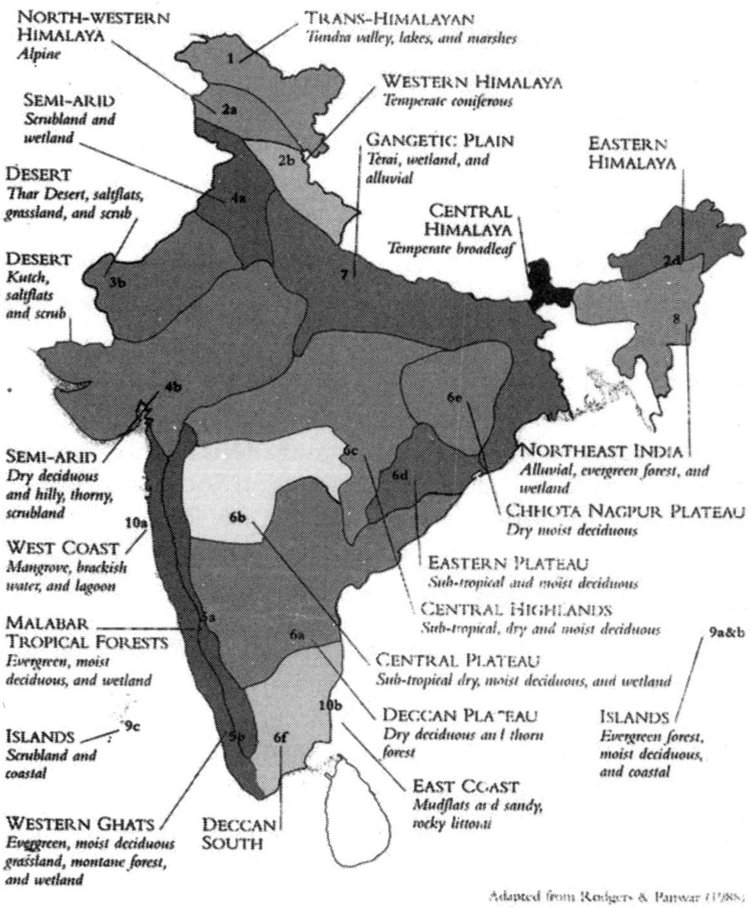

Adapted from Rodgers & Panwar (1988)

has been given top priority and a separate Ministry of Environment & Forests (MOEF) has been entrusted with the task of environmental protection. The Department of Environment (DOE) Forest & wildlife under this ministry has been set up with the view to coordinate between states and the centre and to execute speedy and faithful implementation of the steps to be taken in wild life management in the country.

Aims of Wildlife Management:

1. Protection of Natural habitats
2. Maintenance of the viable number of species in protected areas (PA) National parks, sanctuaries, biosphere reserve.
3. Establishment of Biosphere Reserve for plants and animals.
4. Protection through legislation.
5. Imposing restrictions on export of rare animal species.
6. Improving the existing protected areas as Sanctuaries, national parks etc.
7. Educating the public for environmental protection at all levels.

The governmental and the non-governmental voluntary national organizations and the international organizations like Bombay Natural history society (1883), Wild Life Preservation Society of India (1958) and World Wildlife Fund, India (1969) etc, are keen to protect wild life.

Government Organisations:

A number of wild life acts have been made from time to time, by state as well as Union Government for wildlife Conservation. Some of there are.

1. Madras Wild Elephant Preservation Act, 1873.
2. All-India Elephant Preservation Act, 1879.
3. Assam Rhinoceros Preservation Act, 1954
4. Bengal Rhinoceros Preservation Act, 1932
5. Project Tiger in 1973
6. Gir Asiatic Lion Project in 1972
7. Crocodile Breeding project in 1975
8. Indian Board for wild life in 1952
9. National Wildlife Action Plan, 1982 endorsed by IBWL

10. Wild life (Protection) Act, 1972
11. Indian National Man and the Biosphere Committee, 1972 for Biosphere Reserve.

Why should we conserve endangered species?

The life on earth is inter related and interconnected. Living things depend upon their physical environment – the land, air and water. The plants and vegetation form the basic life – support providers and they also provide food and home for animals, insects and birds. Animals help in dispersal of seeds of plants, and parasites infest plants and animals.

Some wild animals for example, Eagle, hyena, etc. act as scavengers. The bacteria and fungi aid in decomposing the dead. They play an important role in returning the organic and inorganic components of dead animals and plants back to nature to be used and reused by subsequent living organisms.

Nature provides an extremely complex and intricate network of living things delicately balanced and adopted to inhabit the diverse climatic and geographical regions of our plant. Many of these intricate relationships are not understood and so it is very essential to protect the natural wealth of the country.

This is our natural heritage – A heritage we need for sustenance and survival, like the animals and birds.

List of Endangered Mammals

IUCN / WII - 2004

Critically Endangered:

- Jenkin's Shrew (*Crocidura jenkensii*).
- Pygmy Hog (Sus salvanius)
- Wroughton's Free-tailed Bat (*Otomops wroughtoni*)

Endangered:

- Asiatic Black Bear (*Selenarctos thibetanus*)
- Asiatic Lion (*Panthera leo persica*).
- Capped Leaf Monkey (*Trachypithecus pileatus*).
- Golden Leaf Monkey (*Trachypithecus geei*).
- Hispid Hare (*Caprolagus hispidus*).
- Hoolock Gibbon (*Hylobates hoolock*)
- Indian Elephant or Asian Elephant
- Indian Rhinoceros (*Rhinoceros unicornis*).
- Kondana Soft-furred Rat (*Millardia kondana*).
- Lion-tailed Macaque (*Macaca silenus*)
- Malabar Civet (*Viverra civettina*)
- Marsh Mongoose (*Atilax paludinosus)*
- Markhor (*Capra falconeri*).
- Nicobar Tree Shrew (*Tupaia nicobarica*).
- Nicobar Shrew (*Crocidura nicobarica*).
- Nilgiri Leaf Monkey (*Presbytis johni*).
- Nilgiri Tahr (*Hemitragus hylocrius*).
- Particolored Flying Squirrel (*Hylopetes alboniger*).
- Red Panda *(Ailurus fulgens)*
- Servant Mouse (*Mus famulus*).
- Snow Leopard (*Uncia uncia*).
- Tiger (*Panthera tigris*).
- Wild Water Buffalo (*Bubalus bubalis*).

Vulnerable:

1 Asiatic Wild Ass (Equus hemionus Pallas).

1 Blackbuck (Antilope cervicapra).

1 Brown Bear (Ursus arctos)

1 Clouded Leopard (Neofelis nebulosa)

1 Dhole (Cuon alpinus)

1 Gaur (Bos gaurus)

1 Himalayan Musk Deer (Moschus chrysogaster)

1 Himalayan Tahr (Hemitragus jemlahicus)

1 Indian Giant Squirrel (Ratufa indica).

1 Jackal (Canis aureus)

1 Kerala Rat (Rattus ranjiniae)

1 Khajuria's Roundleaf Bat (Hipposideros durgadasi)

1 Himalayan Crestless Porcupine (Hystrix brachyura)

1 Nilgiri Marten (Martes gwatkinsii).

1 Nonsense Rat (Rattus burrus).

1 Palm Rat (Rattus palmarum).

1 Sloth Bear (Melursus ursinus).

1 Slow Loris (Loris tardigradus).

1 Takin (Budorcas taxicolor).

1 Wild Yak (Bos grunniens)

Least Concern :

1 Leopard (*Panthera pardus*)

1 Red Fox (*Vulpes vulpes montana*)

CRITICALLY ENDANGERED

Pygmy Hog

Scientific classification

Kingdom	:	Animalia
Phylum	:	Chordata
Class	:	Mammalia
Order	:	Artiodactyla
Family	:	Suidae
Genus	:	Porcula Hodgson, 1847
Species	:	P. salvania

Binomial name

Porcula salvania (Hodgson, 1847)

Vital Statistics

Range	:	India, Nepal, Bhutan
Weight	:	6.6 – 11.8 Kg
Body Length	:	55 – 71 Cm
Tail Length	:	2.5 Cm
Shoulder Height	:	20 – 30 Cm
Gestation Period	:	About 100 days
Young per birth	:	2 – 6, generally 3 - 4
Diet	:	Roots, grasses, leaves, fruits, insects
Life Span	:	Upto 7.5 years

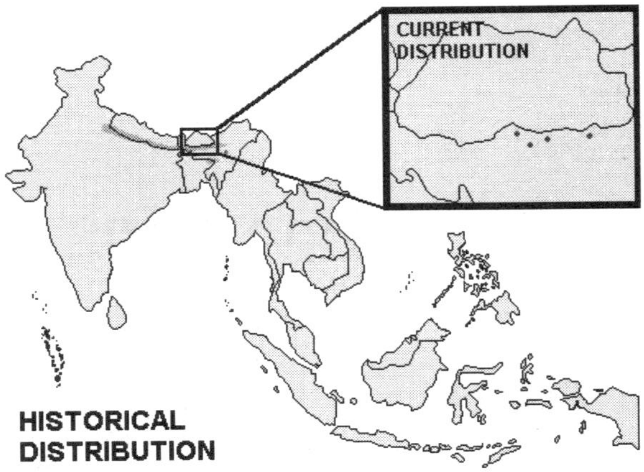

Pygmy hog (Porcula salvania) is an endangered species of small wild pig, previously spread across India, Nepal, and Bhutan but now only found in Assam. The current world population is about 150 individuals or less. Recent conservation measures have increased the prospect of survival in the wild of this critically endangered species.

1. Physical characteristics

They are about 55 to 71 cm long and stand at 20-30 cm with a tail of 2.5 cm. They weigh 6.6 to 11.8 kilograms. Their skin is dark brownish black and the fur is dark. Piglets are born grayish-pink becoming brown with yellow stripes along the body length. The head is sharply tapered and they have a slight crest of hair on the forehead and on the back of the neck. Adult males have the upper canines visible on the sides of the mouth.

2. Status

The Pygmy hog is the sole representative of Porcula, making the conservation of this critically endangered species even more important as its extinction would result in the loss of a unique evolutionary branch of pigs. They used to be widespread in the tall, wet grasslands in the southern Himalayan foothills from Uttar Pradesh to Assam, through Nepal and north Bengal. However, human encroachment has largely destroyed the natural habitat of the pygmy hog by development, agriculture, domestic grazing and deliberate fires.

3. Conservation

Pygmy hog Conservation Programme, PHCP, was established in 1995. the PHCP was established under the umbrella of a formal 'International Conservation Management and Research Agreement' by the Durrell Wildlife Conservation Trust, the IUCN's Pigs, Peccaries and Hippo Specialist group, the Forest Department, Government of Assam, and the Ministry of Environment and Forests, Government of India.

Wroughton's Free-tailed Bat

Scientific classification

Kingdom	:	Animalia
Phylum	:	Chordata
Class	:	Mammalia
Order	:	Chiroptera
Family	:	Molossidae
Genus	:	Otomops
Species	:	O.wroughtoni

Binomial name

Otomops wroughtoni (Thomas, 1913)

Vital Statistics

Size	:	6.3 – 6.7 cm
HBL	:	8.7 - 9.9 cm
Social Unit	:	Groups of 5- 6 to 100s
Habitat	:	One cave (barapeda) in Karnataka
Stratum	:	Aerial, arboreal
Diet	:	Insects

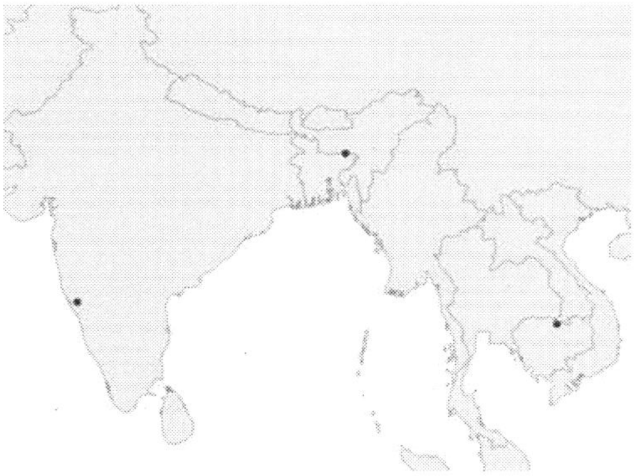

The **Wroughton's Free-tailed Bat** (Otomops wroughtoni) is a free tailed-bat formerly considered to be confined to the Western Ghats area of India. It is listed as a critically endangered species due to habitat loss and a restricted range.

A LARGE, GLOSSY BROWN, critically endangered species, this bat has ears that meet on top of its head. It has a distinct grey collar and small gular sac in both sexes. A small moustache is present beneath circular nostrils.

Adjacent to the Madei Wildlife Sanctuary in Goa, in the state of Karnataka, is Barapede Caves, located between Krishnapur and Talewadi, sole home of Wroughton's Free-tailed Bat, Otomops wroughtoni. Their habitat is threatened by limestone miners, timber contractors and the cave could be submerged if the nearby Madei river were dammed for a hydroelectric plant as proposed by the Karnataka Government.

Jenkin's Shrew

Scientific classification

Kingdom	:	Animalia
Phylum	:	Chordata
Class	:	Mammalia
Order	:	Soricomorpha
Family	:	Soricidae
Genus	:	Crocidura
Species	:	C. jenkinsi

Binomial name

Crocidura jenkinsi (Chakraborty)

Vital Statistics

HBL	:	10.7 cm
Tail	:	10.3 cm

It is Greyish - Brown bristly fur with tail longer than head and body. It is present in South Andaman Island

The **Jenkin's Shrew (Crocidura jenkinsi)** is a species of mammal in the Soricidae family. It is endemic to India.

ENDANGERED

Asiatic Lion

Scientific classification

Kingdom	:	Animalia
Phylum	:	Chordata
Class	:	Mammalia
Order	:	Carnivora
Family	:	Felicidae
Genus	:	Panthera
Species	:	P. leo
Sub Species	:	P.l. persica

Bionomial name

Panthera leo persica (Meyer'1826)

1. Distribution

The Asiatic lion was widespread throughout Southwest Asia. Today the species can only be found in a single location in the wild, the Gir forest in India. Although genetically distinct from the sub-Saharan African lion, the difference is not large. The closeness in genetic make-up between Asiatic and African lions indicates that the two populations got separated as nearly as 100,000 years ago.

Vital Statistics

Range	:	South West Asia
Weight		
Male	:	150 – 250 Kg
Female	:	120 – 180 Kg
Length (Head & Body)	:	

Male	:	1.7 – 2.5 M
Female	:	1.4 – 1.75 M
Tail Length	:	70 – 105 Cm
Shoulder Height		
Male	:	1 – 1.23 M
Female	:	80 – 107 Cm
Sexual Maturity		
Male	:	5 Years
Female	:	4 Years
Mating Season	:	All year round
Gestation Period	:	100 – 119 days
Number of Young	:	1 – 6
Birth Interval	:	18 – 26 Months
Diet	:	Deer, Antelope, Wild Boar, Water Buffalo
Life Span	:	16 – 18 years

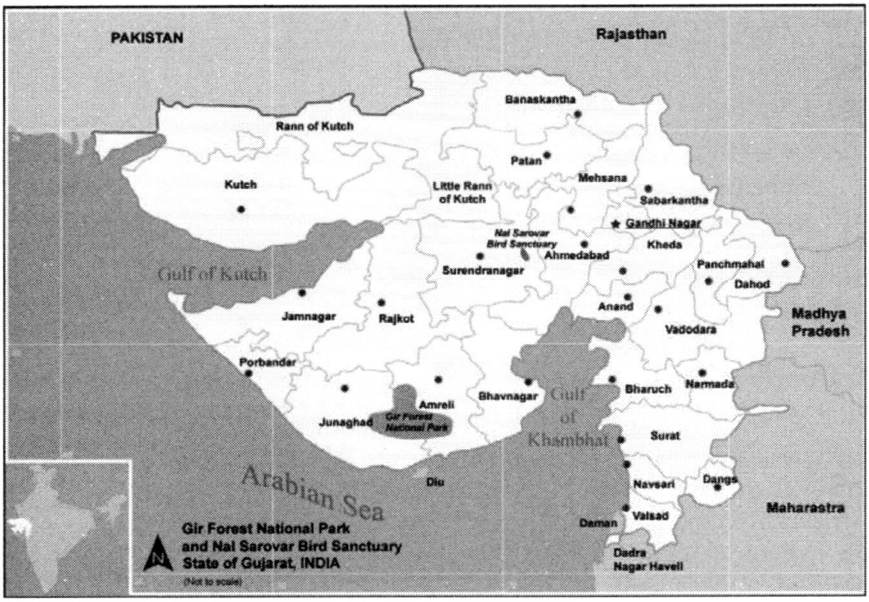

2. Physical Characteristics

The most noticeable physical characteristic found in all Asiatic lions, but rarely in African lions, is a longitudinal fold of skin running along the belly. Also, the mane of the Asiatic lion is generally shorter than that of the African lion, so the ears are always visible. Asiatic lions are, in general, slightly smaller than African lions. Studies on Gir

lions yielded the following figures; adult males weighed 160-190kg, while adult females weighed 110-120 kg. The largest Asiatic lion on record measured 2.9 m from nose to tail-tip.

3. Ecology

Radio-telemetry studies have estimated the mean annual home range for male lions at 110 Km^2, and females at 50 km^2. Male coalitions have ranges between 100-150 km^2 while single males have ranges of comparable size to that of females. Population density is estimated at one lion per 7 km^2

4. Diet

The most commonly taken prey's are the chital and the sambar deer. However, domestic cattle have historically been a major component of the lions' diet.

5. Behaviour

Like their African cousins, Asiatic lions are highly sociable animals living in social units called prides. There are however differences in pride make up between the sub-species. Based on the average number of adult females, the Asiatic pride is smaller. Studies have shown that most Gir prides contain just two adult females as compared to the average African pride which contains 4 to 6 adult females. The largest recorded female coalition of Asiatic lionesses is a group of five. Adult male Asiatic lions exhibit a lesser degree of sociality than African males.

6. Threats

By the middle of this century, with hunting outlawed, the greatest threat to the lion population came from the destruction of its habitat: Vast tracts of jungle forest were cleared to extract wood for commercial use and to make way for the increasing human population. Since their creation in the 1960's , the Gir National Park and Lion Sanctuary have successfully contributed towards the stabilization of the last remaining wild population of Asiatic lions. However, the subspecies is still in great danger of extinction despite these efforts.

7. Conservation

The Indian government then created the Gir national Park and Lion Sanctuary- collectively known as the Gir protected Area (PA), covering over 1000 km^2 . The area is made up of dry scrubland with hills, rivers, and teak forest. In addition to the lion population, the Gir PA contains leopards, antelope, deer, jackals, hyenas, and marsh crocodiles.

At the present time the Gir National Park and Lion Sanctuary is the only place to see Asiatic lions in the wild, and the Indian government has begun to do more to make this unique spectacle visible to tourists and wildlife enthusiasts. Guided jeep safaris through the Gir are available for observing lions.

Indian Rhinoceros

Scientific classification

Kingdom	:	Animalia
Phylum	:	Chordata
Class	:	Mammalia
Order	:	Perissodactyla
Family	:	Rhinocerotidae
Genus	:	Rhinoceros
Species	:	R. unicornis

Binomial name

Rhinoceros unicornis (Linnaeus, 1758)

Vital Statistics

Range	:	India, Nepal, Bhutan
Weight		
Male	:	2200 – 3000 Kg
Female	:	1600 Kg
Length	:	13 feet
Height	:	5.7 – 6.7 feet
Horn Length	:	20 – 101 Cm
Sexual Maturity		
Male	:	9 Years
Female	:	5 Years
Gestation Period	:	16 Months
Young per birth	:	one
Birth Interval	:	3 years
Diet	:	Grasses, leaves, twigs, aquatic plants, fruits
Life Span	:	30 - 45 years

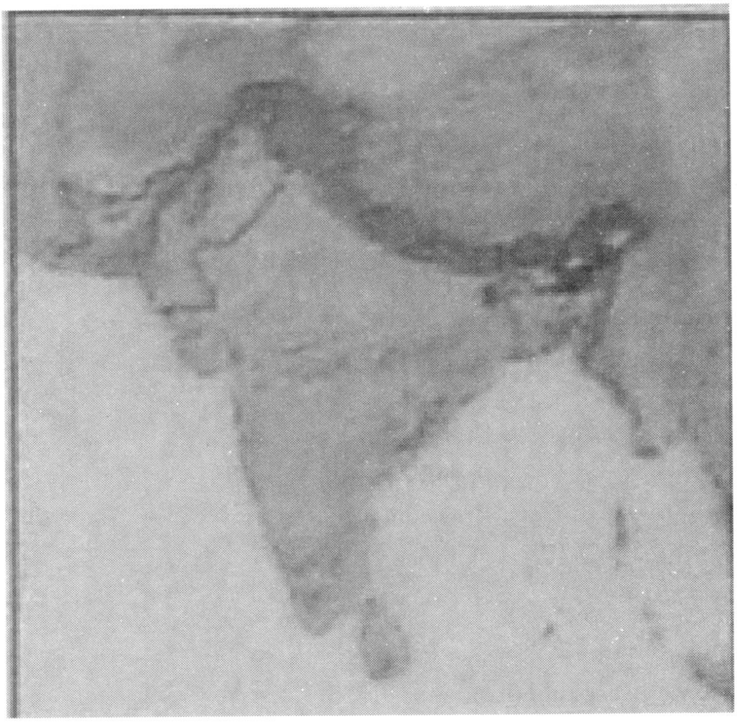

The Indian Rhinoceros or the **Great One-horned Rhinoceros** (Rhinoceros unicornis) is a large mammal found in Nepal and in Assam, India. The Indian Rhinoceros can run at speeds of up to 55 km/h for short periods of time and is also an excellent swimmer. It has an excellent sense of hearing and smell but relatively poor eyesight.

1. Distribution

The rhino once inhabited areas from Pakistan to Burma & Bangladesh and may have even roamed in China. But because of human influence their range has shrunk and now they only exist in small populations in northeastern India and Nepal.

On the former abundance of the species, Thomas C. Jerdon wrote in 1874 in The Mammals of India. That huge rhinoceros is found in the Terai at the foot of the Himalalayas, from Bhotan to Nepal. It is more common in the eastern portion of the Terai than the west, and is most abundant in Assam and the Bhotan Dooars.

2. Physical characteristics

This prehistoric-looking rhinoceros has thick, silver-brown skin which creates huge folds all over its body. Its upper legs and shoulders are covered in wart-like bumps, and has very little body hair. With size equal to that of the white rhino in Africa, it is the fourth-largest land animal, after the three elephant species. Fully grown males are larger than females in the wild, weighing from 2200-3000 kg (4,800 - 6,600 lb). Female Indian rhinos weigh about 1600 kg. The Indian Rhino is from 5.7 to 6.7 feet tall and can be up to 13 feet long. The record-sized specimen of this rhino was approximately 3500 kg. The Great One-Horned Rhinoceros has a single horn; this is present in both males and females, but not on newborn young. The horn, like human fingernails, is pure keratin and starts to show after about 6 years. It reaches a length of between 20 and 101 cm.

3. Diet

Their diet includes grasses, leaves, aquatic plants and fruits. Feeding occurs during the morning and evening where they use their prehensile lip to grasp grass stems. Indian rhinos use lower incisor teeth as a slashing weapon.

4. Behaviour

These rhinos live in tall grasslands and river line forests, but due to habitat loss they have been forced into more cultivated land. They are mostly solitary creatures, with the exception of mothers and calices and breeding pairs, although they sometimes congregate at bathing areas. They have home ranges, the home ranges of males being usually 2-8 square kilometers in size, and overlapping each other. Dominant males tolerate males passing through their territory except when they are in mating season, when dangerous fights breakout. They are active during the day and spend the middle of the day wallowing in lakes, rivers, ponds, and puddles to cool down. They are extremely good swimmers. Over 10 distinct vocalizations have been recorded. Indian rhinos have no natural enemies, except the tigers. Tigers sometimes kill unguarded calves, but adult rhinos are less vulnerable due to their huge size and dangerous horn as a weapons. However, there is a recorded instance of a tiger killing a full-grown female Indian rhino.

5. Threats

This rhino is a major success of conservation. Only 100 remained in the early 1900's and now their population has increased but even so they are still endangered.

The Indian rhino is illegally poached for its horn, which some cultures in East Asia believe has healing and potency powers. Habitat loss is another threat. Fewer than 2500 individuals remain in the wild, and the species is endangered.

6. Conservation

The Indian and Nepalese governments have taken major steps toward Indian Rhinoceros conservation with the help of the World Wildlife Fund (WWF). The Kaziranga National Park and Manas National Park in Assam, Pobiora reserve forest in Assam, Laokhowa reserve forest of Assam having a very small population and Royal Chitwan National Park in Nepal are homes for this endangered animal.

Red Panda

Scientific classification

Kingdom	:	Animalia
Phylum	:	Chordata
Class	:	Mammalia
Subclass	:	Eutheria
Superorder	:	Laurasiatheria
Order	:	Carnivora
Suborder	:	Caniformia
Superfamily	:	Musteloidea
Family	:	Ailuridae
Genus	:	Ailurus
Species	:	A. fulgens

Binomial name

Ailurus fulgens (F. Cuvier, 1825)

Vital Statistics

Range	:	India, Bhutan, China, Myanmar, Nepal
Weight		
Male	:	4.5 – 6.2 Kg
Female	:	3 – 4.5 Kg
Body Length	:	31 – 47 Cm

Tail Length	:	30 – 60 cm
Sexual Maturity	:	2 – 3 Years
Mating Season	:	December - January
Gestation Period	:	112 – 158 days
Diet	:	Berries, fruits, mushrooms, grasses, insects
Life Span	:	8 – 10 years

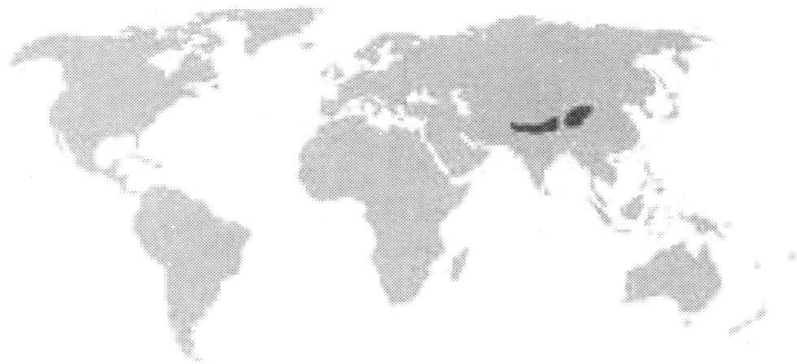

Ailuras fulgens or The Red Panda or Lesser Panda ("shining cat") is a mostly herbivorous mammal, specialized as a bamboo feeder. It is slightly larger than a domestic cat (40-60 cm long, 3-6 kg weight). The Red Panda is endemic to the Himalayas in Bhutan, southern China, India, Laos, Nepal, and Myanmar. Red Panda is the state animal in the Indian state of Sikkim. There is an estimated population of less than 2,500 mature individuals. Their population continues to decline due to habitat fragmentation.

1. Distribution

Red Pandas are native to southeastern Asia, along a crescent formed by the Himalaya Mountain foothills from western Nepal, southern Tibet, Bhutan and Northeast India, then east into the highlands of Myanmar (Burma), the Gongshan Mountains of Yunnan province in China and the Hengduan Mountains of Sichuan province in China.

2. Physical characteristics

The Red Panda is quite long; 79-120 cm, 31 to 47 in (including the tail length of 30 to 60 cm/12 to 24 in). Males weigh 4.5 to 6.2 kg (10 to 14 lb). The Red Panda is specialized as a bamboo feeder, with long and soft reddish-brown fur on upper parts, blackish fur on lower parts, light face with tear markings and robust cranial - dental features .The light face has white badges similar to those of a raccoon, but each individual can have distinctive markings. Its roundest head has medium-sized upright ears, a black nose, and very dark eyes; almost pitch black. Its long bushy tail with six alternating yellowish red transverse ocher rings provides balance and excellent camouflage against its habitat of moss and lichen covered trees. The legs are black, short and bear-like with thick fur on the soles of the paws hiding scent glands and serving as thermal insulation on snow-covered or ice surfaces. The Red Panda is specialized as a bamboo feeder with strong, curved and sharp semi-retractile claws standing inward for firm grasping to facilitate substantial movement on narrow tree branches and seizing leaves and fruit. Like the Giant Pandas (Ailuropoda melanoleuca), it has a "false thumb" that really is an extension of the wrist bone.

3. Diet

The Red Panda eats mostly bamboo. Like the Giant Panda, it cannot digest cellulose, so it must consume a large volume of bamboo to survive. Its diet consists of about two-thirds bamboo, but they also eat berries, fruit, mushrooms, roots, acorns, lichen, grasses and they are known to supplement their diet with young birds, eggs, small rodents, and insects on occasion.

4. Behaviour

Red Pandas are crepuscular (most active at dawn and dusk) and live in the slopes of the south of the Himalayas and the mountainous forests of the southwest of China, at altitudes of up to 4,800 meters, and generally do not venture below 1,800 meters. They are sedentary during the day resting in the branches of trees and in tree hollows and increase their activity only in the late afternoon and/or early evening hours. They are very heat sensitive with an optimal "well-being" temperature between 17 and 25 degree C, and cannot tolerate temperatures over 25 degree C at all. Red Pandas are very skillful and acrobatic animals that live predominantly in trees. They live in territorities, frequently as loners, and only rarely live in pairs or in groups of families. They are very quiet except for some twittering and whistling communication sound. Red Pandas drink by plunging their paw into the water and licking their paws

5. Threats

Red Pandas begin their daily activity with a ritual washing of their fur by licking their front paws and massaging their back, stomach and sides. They also scrub their back and belly along the sides of trees or a rock. They then patrol their territory, marking it with a strong musk-smelling secretion from their anal gland and with their urine. No reliable numbers exist for the total population but it is very threatened due to the fragmentation of its natural habitats, their small numbers and their food specialization needs. In Southwest China the Red Panda is hunted for its fur and especially for its highly-valued bushy tail from which hats are produced. In the areas of China, where the Red Panda lives, their fur is often used for local cultural ceremonies and in weddings the bridegroom traditionally carries the hide. The 'good -luck charm' hats are used by Chinese newlyweds. The continuous clearing of the forests, has significantly reduced the population. It is now protected in all countries in which it lives, and the hunting of Red Pandas is illegal everywhere. Nevertheless, poaching continues and they are often illegally hunted and sold to zoos for removal prices. The IUCN has mandated that small Pandas are a "threatened species" since 1996.

Tiger

Scientific classification

Kingdom	:	Animalia
Phylum	:	Chordata
Class	:	Mammalia
Order	:	Carnivora
Family	:	Felidae
Genus	:	Panthera
Species	:	P.tigris

Binomial name

Panthera tigris (Linnaeus, 1758)

Vital Statistics

Range	:	India, Bangladesh, Bhutan, Myanmar
Weight		
Male	:	205 – 227 Kg
Female	:	141 Kg
Body Length	:	6 – 9 feet
Tail Length	:	3 feet
Sexual Maturity		3 – 4 years
Mating Season	:	All year round
Gestation Period	:	16 weeks
Young per birth	:	3 – 4
Diet	:	Deer, Wild Buffalo, elephant, wild pigs, cattle and sometime human
Life Span	:	8 - 15 years

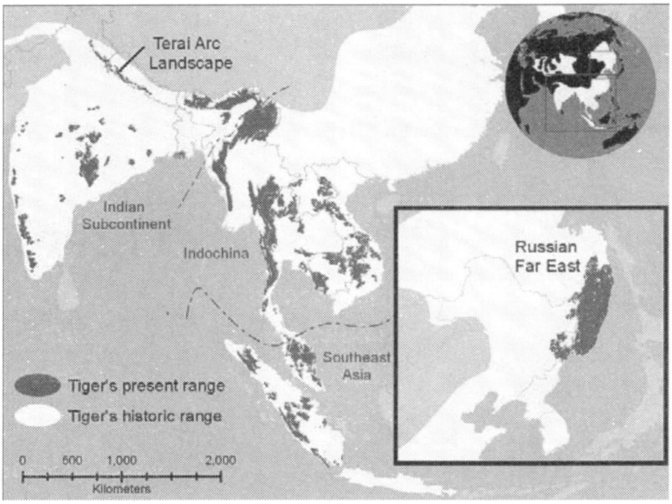

The Tiger (Panthera tigris) is a mammal of the Felidae family, the largest of four "big cats" in the Panthera genus. . Native to the mainland of Asia, the tiger is an apex predator and the largest feline species in the world, comparable in size to the biggest fossil felids. The Bengal tiger is the most common subspecies of tiger, constituting approximately 80% of the entire tiger population, and is found in India, Bangladesh, and Bhutan.

1. Physical characteristics

Tigers are the heaviest cats found in the wild, but the subspecies differ strongly in size, tending to increase proportionally with latitude, as predicted by Bergmann's Rule.

Tigers have rusty-reddish to brown-rusty coats, a fair (whitish) medial and ventral area and stripes that vary from brown or hay to pure black. The form and density of stripes differs between subspecies, but most tigers have over 100 stripes. The pattern of stripes is unique to each animal, and thus could potentially be used to identify individuals, much in the same way as fingerprints are used to identify people. This is not, however, a preferred method of identification, due to the difficulty of recording the stripe pattern of a wild tiger. It seems likely that the function of stripes is camouflage, serving to hide these animals from their prey. The stripe pattern is found on a tiger's skin and if shaved, its distinctive camouflage pattern would be preserved.

2. Habitat

Tigers are found in a variety of habitats, including both tropical and evergreen forests, woodlands, grasslands, rocky country, swamps, and savannas. The Caspian tiger was also found in steppes and mountainous areas. Compared to the lion, the tiger prefers more dense vegetation, for which its camouflage is ideally suited, and where a single predator is not a disadvantage compared to a pride. Among the big cats, only the tiger and jaguar are strong swimmers; tigers are often found bathing in ponds, lakes, and rivers.

3. Diet

In the wild, tigers mostly feed on larger and medium sized animals. Sambar, guar, water buffalo, chital, wild boar and nilgai are the tiger's favored prey in India. They also may kill such formidable predators as dholes, leopards, and pythons. Tigers have been known to kill even crocodiles on occasion, although predation is rare and the predators typically avoid one another. Adult elephants are too dangerous to tigers to serve as common prey, but conflicts between elephants and tigers do sometimes take place. A case where a tiger killed an adult female Indian rhino has been observed. Young elephant and rhino calves are occasionally taken. Tigers also sometimes prey on domestic animals such as dogs, cows, horses and donkeys. These individuals are termed cattle-lifters or cattle-killers in contrast to typical game.

4. Behaviour

Male tigers can mingle easily with females in their territories and will even share kills. George Schaller observed a male tiger share a kill with two females and four cubs. Females are often reluctant to let males near their cubs, but Schaller saw that these females made no effort to protect or keep their cubs from the male. This suggests that the male might have been the father of the cubs.

5. Sunderbans Man-eaters

While killings by Siberian tigers are almost unheard of, the Bengal tigers of the Sunderbans (translation: 'beautiful forest') India and Bangladesh, used to kill regularly sixty people a year. This was strange given that the tigers were usually in prime condition and had adequate prey available. Approximately 600 tigers live in this region, the largest population anywhere in the world.. It is necessary to place these attacks in perspective. Firstly, the kill rate has dropped significantly due to better management techniques and now only about three people lose their lives each year. Even at the rate of fifty or sixty kills per year kills would only provide about 3 % of the yearly food requirements for the tiger population of the Sunderbans. Therefore, despite the notoriety associated with this area, man is only a supplement to the tiger's diet; they do not provide a primary food source.

6. Conservation

Humans are the tiger's most significant predator, as tigers are often poached illegally for their fur. Many Indian tigers' parts found their way to Tibet, where they were widely used for making traditional costumes. Tiger conservation efforts in India, which harbors the largest population of wild tigers in the world, have also been underway, though are also continually threatened by poachers. Poaching for fur and destruction of habitat has greatly reduced tiger populations in the wild. A century ago, it is estimated there were over 100,000 tigers in the world but the population has dwindled to between 7,000 and 5,000 tigers. Some breeding estimates suggest the population is even lower, with some at less than 2,500 mature breeding individuals, with no subpopulation containing more than 250 mature breeding individuals. The threat of extinction is mitigated somewhat by the presence of some 20,000 tigers currently in captivity, although parts of the captive population (eg. The 5-5,000 animals in China's commercial tiger farms) is of very low genetic diversity and can be of little use in keeping the species alive.

Markhor

Scientific classification

Kingdom	:	Animalia
Phylum	:	Chordata
Class	:	Mammalia
Order	:	Artiodactyla
Family	:	Bovidae
Subfamily	:	Caprinae
Genus	:	Capra
Species	:	C. falconeri

Binomial name

Capra falconeri (Wagner, 1839)

Vital Statistics

Range	:	India
Weight	:	52 - 110 Kg
Length	:	132 - 186 Cm
Tail Length	:	8 – 20 Cm
Shoulder Height	:	65 – 115 Cm
Gestation Period	:	135 – 175 days
Sexual Maturity	:	18 – 30 months
Mating Season	:	Winter
Young per birth	:	1 - 2
Diet	:	Leaves, grasses, twigs
Life span	:	12 – 13 years

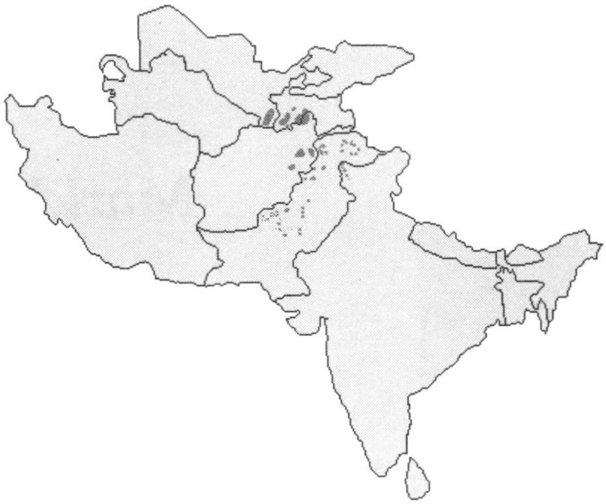

The Markhor (Capra falconeri) is a goat-antelope found in sparse woodland in the Western Himalayas.

Physical characteristics

Females are tan in colour with the same white underbelly and pattern of black and white on the legs. Males have a lighter tan colour with the same white underbelly and pattern on the legs, as well as a black face and large amount of long shaggy white fur on their neck and chest which can grow to knee-length. Both sexes have corkscrew-shaped horns which can grow up to 160 cm/ 64 inches long in males, and up to 25 cm / 10 inches in females.

Habitat

Markhor are found at altitudes of 500 to 3500 meters (1,500 to 11,000 feet) where they eat grass, leaves, and whatever other vegetative matter they can find. They are often found standing on their hind legs to reach the top leaves of trees. Markhor are crepuscular, active in the early morning and late afternoon. Females gather in herds of up to nine individuals and males are normally solitary. During mating season, males fight each other for the attention of females. These fights involve lunging until the two males' horns are locked together, and then twisting and pushing until one male falls. Markhor sound much like the domestic goat.

Hoolock Gibbon

Scientific classification

Kingdom	:	Animalia
Phylum	:	Chordata
Class	:	Mammalia
Order	:	Primates
Family	:	Hylobatidae
Genus	:	Hoolock
Species	:	Hoolock hoolock

Binomial name

Hoolock hoolock (Harlan,1834)

Vital Statistics

Range	:	India, Myanmar
Weight		6 – 9 Kg
Length	:	60 – 90 Cm
Sexual Maturity		6 - 8 years
Mating Season	:	March - May
Social Unit Groups	:	2 - 3
Gestation Period	:	7 Months
Diet	:	Fruits, insects, leaves
Life Span	:	25 years
Stratum	:	Arboreal

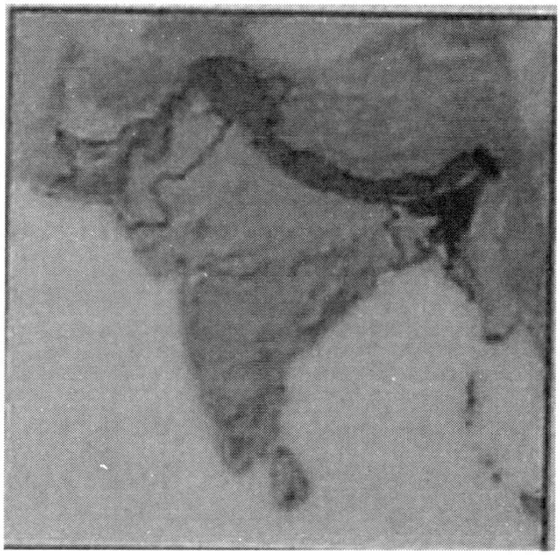

1. Physical characteristics

Hoolocks are the second largest of the gibbons, after the Siamang. They reach a size of 60 to 90 cm and weigh 6 to 9 kg. the genders are about the same size, but they differ considerably in coloration: males are black colored with remarkable white brows, while females have a grey-brown fur, which is darker at the chest and neck. White rings around the eyes and around the mouth give their face a mask-like appearance. One unique aspect of gibbon physiology is that the wrist is composed of a ball and socket joint, allowing for biaxial movement. This greatly reduces the amount of energy needed in the upper arm and torso, while also reducing stress on the shoulder joint. They also have long hands and feet, with a deep cleft between the first and second digits of their hands. Some species have an enlarged throat sac, which inflates and serves as a resonating chambers when the animals call. This structure is enormous in a few species, equaling the size of the animal's head.

2. Ecology & Habitat

The range of the hoolocks is the most northwestern, extending from Assam in North-East India to Myanmar. Small populations (in each case few hundred animals) live also in the eastern Bangladesh and in southwest China. Like the other gibbons, they are diurnal and arboreal, brachiating through the trees with their long arms. Their diet consists mainly of fruits, insects and leaves. Gibbons are social

animals. They are strongly territorial, and defend their boundaries with vigorous visual and vocal displays. The vocal element, which can often be heard for distances of up to 1 km, consists of a duet between a mated pair, their young sometimes joins in. In most species, males, and in some also females sing solos that attract mates as well as advertise their territory.

3. Behaviour

They live together in monogamous pairs. They stake out a territory and their calls serve to locate family members and ward off other gibbons from their territory.

4. Status

Most species are threatened or endangered, most importantly from degradation or loss of their forest habitat.

Golden Leaf Monkey

Scientific classification

Kingdom	:	Animalia
Phylum	:	Chordata
Class	:	Mammalia
Order	:	Primates
Family	:	Cercopithecidae
Genus	:	Trachypithecus
Species group	:	T. pileatus
Species	:	T.geei

Binomial name

Trachypithecus geei (Khajuria, 1956)

Gee's Golden Languor (Trachypithecus geei), or simply the Golden Languor, is an Old World monkey found in a small region of western Assam, India and in the neighboring foothills of the Black mountains of Bhuttan.

1. Physical characteristics

The golden Langur is known for its rich golden to bright ceramic hair, a black face and a very long tail measuring up to 50 cm in length. For the most part, the languor is confined to high trees where its long tail serves as a balancer when its leaps across branches. During the rainy season it obtains water from dew and rain drenched leaves.

2. Diet

Its diet is herbivorous, consisting of ripe and unripe fruits, mature and young leaves, seeds, buds and flowers.

3. Habitat and Behaviour

The region of its distribution is very small, limited to the area bounded on the south by the Brahmaputra river, on the east by the Manas river, on the west by the Sankosh river, all in Assam, India, and on the north by the Black mountains of Bhutan· It generally lives in troops of about 8 (but sometimes upto 50) with several females to each adult male.

4. Status

The Golden Langur is currently endangered; the total Indian population in 2001 was recorded to be 1,064 individuals, with the relative dearth of infants and juveniles indicating a declining population and with the habitat being degraded by human activity.

Snow Leopard

Scientific classification

Kingdom	:	Animalia
Phylum	:	Chordata
Class	:	Mammalia
Order	:	Carnivora
Family	:	Felidae
Subfamily	:	Pantherinae
Genus	:	Panthera
Species	:	P. uncial

Binominal name

Panthera uncial (Schreber, 1775)

Vital Statistics

Range	:	Central and Southern Asia
Weight		35 - 55 Kg
Body Length	:	4 feet
Tail Length	:	3 feet
Height	:	2 feet
Young per birth	:	1 - 3
Diet	:	Goat, sheep, deer, wild pigs
Life Span	:	15 - 18 years

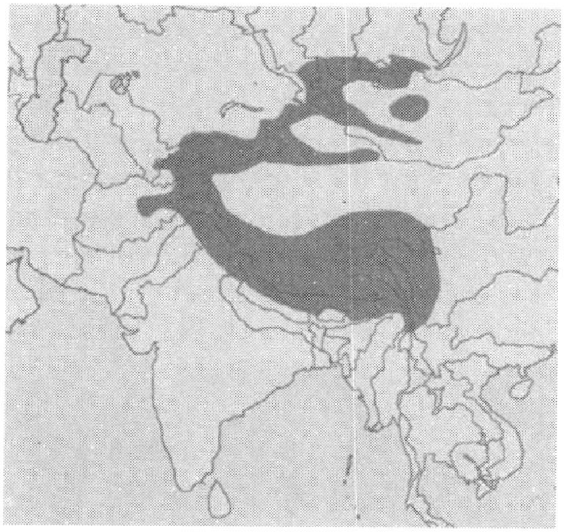

The Snow Leopard (Panthera uncial or Uncia uncial), sometimes known as the Ounce, is a large cat native to the mountain ranges of central and southern Asia.

1. Distribution

The Snow Leopard's range in central and south Asia is rugged mountainous regions of approximately 1,230,000 square kilometers, which extends through 12 countries: Afghanistan, Bhutan, Tibet, India, Kazakhstan, the Kyrgyz Republic, Mongolia, Nepal, Pakistan, Russia, Tajikistan and Uzbekistan. The total estimated wild population of the Snow Leopard is between 4,000 and 7,500 individuals (see table below). In addition, there are 600-700 animals in zoos around the world.

Range Country	Habitat Area	Estimated Population
India	75,000	200 - 600

An individual Snow Leopard lives within a well defined home range. However, it does not defend its range aggressively when encroached upon by other individuals. The Snow Leopard needs over 1,000 km^2 to survive.

2. Physical characteristics

The Snow leopard has grey-and-white fur with numerous rosettes on the flanks and spots on the head and neck, similar to the Jaguar. Its tail is striped and can reach up to 90cm long. It is an opportunistic feeder, eating whatever meat it can find; it often kills animals three times its size, including domestic livestock. It ambushes prey from above when possible, as it can jump as far as 14 meters (46 feet). Its agility often proves helpful when ambushing prey and traversing through mountains. The Snow leopard can be distinguished from other similar species by its proportionately longer tail, which helps it maintain its balance on the rugged terrain and unstable surfaces of its habitat. The Snow leopard's tail also doubles as warmth cover and is used to cover its nose and mouth in very cold conditions. The male's head is usually much squarer and wider than that of the female. Its big furry feet act as snowshoes, like those of the lynxes.

3. HABITAT

In summer, the Snow Leopard usually lives above the three lines on mountainous meadows and rocky regions at an altitude of up to 6000 m. In winter, it comes down into the forests at an altitude of about 2000 m. It leads largely a solitary life, although mothers can rear cubs for extended periods of time in cave dens in the mountains.

4. Conservation

Snow Leopard in the San Diego Zoo

The Snow Leopard is an endangered species whose pelts command a very high price in the fur market. During the 1960s, the Snow

Leopard's total population went down to 1,000 animals, but has since recovered slightly.

Protected Areas:

- Hemis National Park, in east Ladakh, India.
- Valley of Flowers National Park, Uttaranchal, India, a UNESCO Natural World Heritage Site.

Much progress has been made in securing the survival of the Snow Leopard, with Snow Leopards being successfully bred in captivity. The animals usually give birth to 2 to 3 cubs in a litter, but can give birth to up to 7 in some cases.

Nilgiri Tahr

Scientific classification

Kingdom	:	Animalia
Phylum	:	Chordata
Class	:	Mammalia
Order	:	Artiodactyla
Family	:	Bovidae
Subfamily	:	Caprinae
Genus	:	Nilgiritragus
Species	:	N. hylocrius

Binomial name

Nilgiritragus hylocrius (Ogilby, 1838)

Vital Statistics

Range	:	India (mostly southern)
Weight (Male)		80 – 100 Kg
Shoulder Height	:	100 Cm
Horn Length		
Male	:	40 Cm
Female	:	30 Cm
Diet	:	Grasses, leaves

1. Distribution

The Nilgiri Tahr (Nilgiritragus hylocrius) ungulate native to the Nilgiri hills and the southern portion of the Western Ghats range in Tamil Nadu and Kerala states of southernmost India. It is known locally as the Nilgiri ibex or simply ibex.

2. Physical characteristics

The Nilgiri Tahr are stocky goats with short, coarse fur and a bristly mane. Males are larger than the females, and have a darker color when mature. Both sexes have curved horns, which are larger in the males, reaching up to 40 cm for males and 30 cm for females. Adult males weigh 80-100 kg and stand about 100cm tall at the shoulder.

3. Ecology and Habitat

The tahrs inhabit the open montage grassland habitat of the South Western ghat montage rainforests ecoregion. At elevations from 1200 to 2600 m (generally above 2000m), the forests open into grasslands interspersed with pockets of stunted forests, known as sholos. These grassland habitats and are surrounded by dense forests at the lower elevations. The Nilgiri Tahrs formerly ranged over these grasslands in large herds.

4. Threats & Conservation

But hunting and poaching in the nineteenth century reduced their population to as few as 100 animals by the early 20th century. Since that time their populations have increased somewhat, and presently number about 2000 individuals. Their range extends over 400 km from north to South, and Eravikulam National Park is home to the largest population. The other significant concentration is in the Nilhir hills, with smaller populations in the Anamalai hills, Periyar National Park, Palni hills and other pockets in the Western Ghats south of Eravikulam, almost to India's southern tip.

Kondana Soft - Furred Rat

Scientific classification

Kingdom	:	Animalia
Phylum	:	Chordata
Class	:	Mammalia
Order	:	Rodentia
Family	:	Muridae
Genus	:	Millardia
Species	:	M. kondana

Binomial name

Millardia kondana (Mishra & Dhanda, 1975)

Vital Statistics

Habitat : Endemic to Pune District, Maharshtra

This is a soft furred rat very similar but larger than Millardia meltada. (soft furred field rat)

The Kondan Soft-furred Rat (Millardia kondana) is a species of rodent in the Muridae family. It is found only in India. Its natural habitats are subtropical and tropical dry forests, subtropical or tropical dry lowland, grassland and urban areas.

Servant Mouse

Scientific classification

Kingdom	:	Animalia
Phylum	:	Chordata
Class	:	Mammalia
Order	:	Rodentia
Family	:	Muridae
Genus	:	Mus
Species	:	M. famulus

Binomial name

Mus famulus (Bonhote, 1898)

Vital Statistics

Size HBL	:	9 cm
Tail	:	8 cm
Habitat and occurrence	:	Endemic to W Ghats (around 1,500 m)

A medium sized brown field mouse with a tail that is shorter than head and body length, the Bonhote's Mouse has dark brown feet and a light brown ventral side. The female has three pairs of mammae.

The servant Mouse (Mus famulus) is species of rodent in the Muridae family. It is found only in India. Its natural habitats are subtropical and tropical dry forests, subtropical or tropical dry lowland, grassland. It is threatened by habitat loss.

Particolored Flying Squirrel

Scientific classification

Kingdom	:	Animalia
Phylum	:	Chordata
Class	:	Mammalia
Order	:	Rodentia
Family	:	Sciuridae
Genus	:	Hylopetes
Species	:	H. alboniger

Binomial name

Hylopetes alboniger (Hodgson, 1836)

Vital Statistics

Range	:	Sikkim, North Bengal, NE India
Identification	:	Black and White Squirrel, hoary upper parts

The Particolored Flying Squirrel (Hylopetes alboniger) is a species of rodent in the Sciuridae family. It is found in Bangladesh, Bhutan, Cambodia, China, Laos, Myanmar, Nepal, Thailand, and Vietnam. Its natural habitat is subtropical or tropical dry forests. It is threatened by habitat loss.

Nicobar Shrew

Scientific classification

Kingdom	:	Animalia
Phylum	:	Chordata
Class	:	Mammalia
Order	:	Soricomorpha
Family	:	Soricidae
Genus	:	Crocidura
Species	:	C. nicobarica

Binomial name

Crocidura nicobarica (Miller, 1902)

Vital Statistics

Occurrence	:	Great Nicobar Island
Identification	:	Sooty Brown, Bristly dorsal fur
HBL	:	10.7 – 12 cm
Tail	:	9 – 9.5 cm

The Nicobar Shrew or Nicobar White-tailed Shrew (Crocidura nicobarica) is a species of mammal in the Soricidae family. It is endemic to India.

Nicobar Tree shrew

Scientific classification

Kingdom	:	Animalia
Phylum	:	Chordata
Class	:	Mammalia
Order	:	Scandentia
Family	:	Tupaiidae
Genus	:	Tupaia
Species	:	T. nicobarica

Binomial name

Tupaia nicobarica (Zelebor,1869)

The Nicobar Tree shrew (Tupaia nicobarica) is species of tree shrew in the Tupaiidae family. It is endemic in India. Its natural habitat is subtropical or tropical dry forests. It is threatened by habitat loss.

Capped Leaf Monkey

Scientific classification

Kingdom	:	Animalia
Phylum	:	Chordata
Class	:	Mammalia
Order	:	Primates
Family	:	Cercopithecidae
Genus	:	Trachypithecus
Species	:	T. pilleatus

Binomial name

Trachypithecus pilleatus (Blyth, 1843)

Range	:	India, Bangladesh, China, Myanmar
Length	:	60 – 70 Cm
Tail Length	:	75 – 100 Cm
Weight	:	12 Kg
Mating Season	:	Winter
Diet	:	Leaves, fruits

Vital Statistics

The Bonneted Langur, Capped Langur, Capped Leaf Monkey, or Capped Monkey (Trachypithecus pilleatus) is a species of primate in the Cercopithedae family. It is found in Bangladesh, China, India and Myanmar. Its natural habitat is subtropical or tropical dry forests. It is threatened by habitat loss.

Distinctive Characters :

A cap or crown of erect, long, coarse hairs directed backwards from the forehead gives this monkey its name. Its slender graceful build distinguishes it from the macaques, while its colour distinguishes it from other langurs. The dark-grey colouring of its back and limbs contrasts sharply with the pale fulvous, orange or golden red of the cheeks and underparts. Newborn young have been described as golden, golden red and creamy white. Other langurs are black at birth.

Distribution :

Assam to the adjoining districts of Chittagong and upper Burma. Four races distinctive in details of colour inhabit the hill ranges of Assam. A fifth occurs in Burma

Habits :

The Capped Langur or Leaf Monkey lives in the dense forests which cover the hills of Assam and the Indo-Burma border. The troops keep to the trees and, it is said, seldom come to ground even to drink from the numerous streams which flow through their habitat. They take their water from dew or rain-drenched leaves. Like all langurs they are vegetarians, restricting their food to fruit, flowers, and leaves. As forest dwellers, they are shy and wary, quick to take flight or screen themselves behind foliage in the way langurs do. The alarm note is a sharp guttural bark. The only other vocal sounds noted are likened to squealing. Little is known of the social life of these monkeys. During the cold weather troops consisting of a male overlord, three or four wives and their immature young have been observed. Troops consisting exclusively of males, probably those temporarily expelled from harems, have been seen. All this suggests a social life similar to that of our Common Langur. The time when breeding activity is especially marked is during the cold weather. The period of gestation is not known, nor do we know how long these monkeys take to become fully adult.

Hispid Hare

Scientific classification

Kingdom	:	Animalia
Phylum	:	Chordata
Class	:	Mammalia
Order	:	Lagomorpha
Family	:	Leporidae
Genus	:	Carprolagus
Species	:	C. hispidus

Binomial name

Carprolagus hispidus (Pearson, 1839)

Vital Statistics

Range	:	India
Length	:	30 - 50 Cm
Weight	:	2 – 2.5 Kg
Young per birth	:	2 - 5
Diet	:	Shoots and roots of grass
Size	:	40 – 50 cm
Habitat and Occurrence	:	Terai grassland and forests of the Himalayan foothills in Assam, West Bengal and Uttar Pradesh
Behaviour	:	Smaller home range than other hares. Its pellets are normally seen near thatch cuttings
Best Seen	:	at Manas NP (Assam)

The Hispid Hare, Carprolagus hispidus, is a leporid native to the foot hills of the Himalaya. A large grassland lagomorph of northeastern India, the Hispid Hare or Assam Rabbit is critically endangered. It has black hair mixed into its predominantly brown dorsal coat and has a rufous chest and white belly. It has shorter and more rounded ears, and smaller hind legs than the Indian Hare. It is a slow moving creature and its droppings are rounded, unlike the slightly tapered pellets of the Blacknaped hare.

This hare was formerly widely distributed but its habitat is much reduced and degraded by deforestation, cultivation and human settlement, and now it is confined to isolated regions in Uttar Pradesh, Bihar, West Bengal and Assam. It is one of the world's rarest mammals. Other names include Bristly Rabbit and Assam Rabbit.

Lion - Tailed Macaque

Scientific classification

Kingdom	:	Animalia
Phylum	:	Chordata
Class	:	Mammalia
Order	:	Primates
Family	:	Cercopithecidae
Genus	:	Macaca
Species	:	M. silenus

Binomial name

Macaca silenus (Linnaeus, 1758)

The Lion -tailed Macaque (Macaca silenus) is an Old World monkey that lives only in the Western Ghats of South India.

Vital Statistics

Range	:	India
Weight	:	3 – 10 Kg
Length	:	45 – 60 Cm
Sexual Maturity		
Male	:	6 Years
Female	:	4 Years
Gestation Period	:	6 Months
Diet	:	Fruits, leaves, buds, insects
Life Span	:	20 years

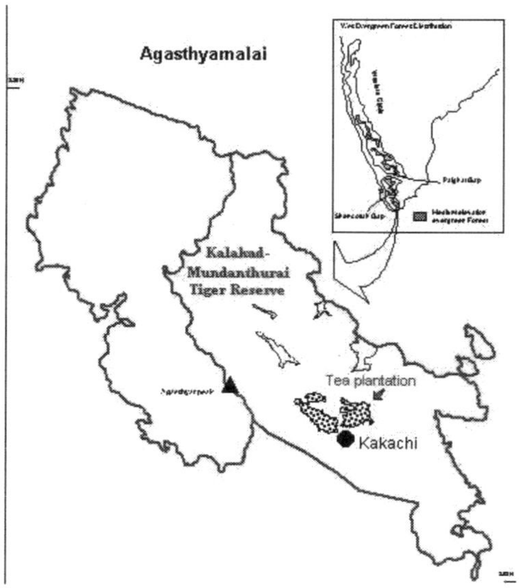

1. Distribution

According to the IUCN, only approximately 2,500 of these animals live scattered over several areas in Karnataka, Kerala and Tamil Nadu. The Lion-tailed macaque ranks among the rarest and most threatened primates. Their range has become increasingly isolated and fragmented by the spread of agriculture and tea, coffee, teak and cinchona, construction of water reservoirs for irrigation and power generation, and human settlements to support such activities. Destruction of their habitat and the fact that they avoid human proximity, have led to the drastic decrease of their population.

2. Physical characteristics

The fur of the Lion-tailed Macaque is dark-brown or black. Its outstanding characteristic is the silver-white mane which surrounds the head from the cheeks down to its chin, and it which gives this monkey its German name of "Beard Ape"

3. Diet

The Lion-tailed macaque behaviour is characterized by typical patterns such as arboreal living, selectively feeding on a large variety of fruit trees, large inter-individual spaces while foraging, and time budgets with high proportion of time devoted to exploration and feeding. The Lion-tailed Macaque primarily eat indigenous fruits, leaves, buds, insects and small vertebrates in virgin forest but can adapt to rapid environmental change in areas of massive selective logging through behavioral modifications and broadening of food choices to include fruits, seeds, shoots, pith, flower, cone, mesocarp, and other parts of many non indigenous and pioneer plants

4. Behaviour

The Lion-tailed Macaque is a diurnal rain forest dweller. It is a good climber and spends a majority of its life in the upper canopy of tropical moist evergreen forests. Unlike other macaques, it avoids humans. In group behaviour, it is much like other macaques : it lives in hierarchical groups of usually ten to twenty animals, which consist of few males and many females. It is a territorial animal, defending its area first with loud cries towards the invading troops. If this proves fruitless, it brawls aggressively.

5. Conservation

During 1993 to 1996, fourteen troops of Lion-tailed macaque were observed in Silent Valley National Park, Kerala, one of the most undisturbed viable habitats left for the Lion-tailed macaque. A local census concluded in 2007, conducted in the Theni District of Tami Nadu, put their numbers at around 250, which was considered encouraging, because till then, there had not been any records of Lion-tailed macaques in that specific area .Many zoos take part in breeding programs which help to secure the survival of this species. 368 of this Macaque are reported to live in zoos.

Malabar Civet

Scientific classification

Kingdom	:	Animalia
Phylum	:	Chordata
Class	:	Mammalia
Order	:	Carnivora
Family	:	Viverridae
Genus	:	Viverra
Species	:	V. civettina

Binomial name

Viverra civettina (Blyth, 1862)

The Malabar civet is endemic to the Western Ghats. It is mostly recorded from the coastal district of Western Ghats in Southern India.

Vital Statistics

Range	:	South India
Weight	:	6.45 – 8 Kg
Body length	:	1090 – 1250 mm
Tail Length	:	330 – 440 mm
Diet	:	Small mammals, reptiles, amphibians, fishes, birds eggs and some vegetables
Social Unit	:	Solitary
Size	:	125 cm

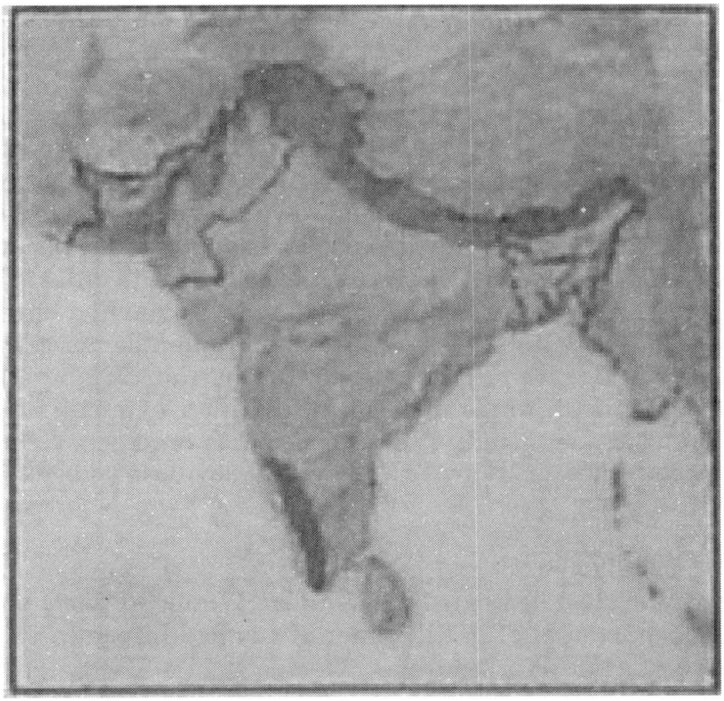

1. Physical characteristics

It is a large civet, almost similar in size to the large Indian civet V. zibetha. It exact measurement is not available. However, it is believed that an adult is around 1090-1250 mm long including tail which is around 330 to 400 mm and weighing up to 6.45 to 8 kg. The coat is long and full grey in color. The body pattern is blackish and larger in size as compared to the little civet. The dorsal crest is black and prominent extending from neck up to the tip of the tail. The tail has five white rings, the last one being only about two inches from the tip.

2. Habitat & Ecology

The Malabar large spotted civet's original habitat was found in the Malabar Coast moist forests belt below the Western Ghats, where it lived in wooded plains and adjoining hill slopes. It was once very common in the coastal districts of Malabar and Travancore. Extensive deforestation has reduced a Malabar forests to a series of isolated patches. Cashew plantations are a refuge, which probably hold most of the surviving populations of Malabar civet and are now threatened by large-scale clearance for rubber plantations.

3. Behaviour

The Malabar civet once inhabited the lowland forests in its range. In northern Kerala it appears to be confined to thickets in cashew plantations, and to highly degraded lowland forests. It is reported to be nocturnal and retreats to the scrub forests and cashew plantations during the day for shelter. The nocturnal cats are carnivorous, solitary and aggressive in nature. They forage on the ground and have been observed in trees. It feeds on small mammals, reptiles, amphibians, fishes, birds eggs and some vegetable matter. The species is reportedly difficult to maintain in captivity for extracting civet, a secretion from anal glands of all civets that is used as a stabilizing agent in perfumes, in oriental medicine and flavouring 'beedis' (local cigarettes).

4. Conservation Status

It is listed in Schedule I part I of the Indian Wildlife (Protection) Act, 1972, Appendix I of CITES, CR C2a in IUCN Red List and CR A 1 be during the CAMP Workshop

5. Threats

The major threat facing isolated populations that have managed to survive in marginal habitats is changing cash crop practices and accidental hunting with dogs. They tend to be treated as raiders of poultry and are captured and killed when encountered.

Marsh Mongoose

Scientific classification

Kingdom	:	Animalia
Phylum	:	Chordata
Class	:	Mammalia
Order	:	Carnivora
Family	:	Herpestidae
Subfamily	:	Herpestinae
Genus	:	Atilax
Species	:	A. paludinosus

Binomial name

Atilax paludinosus (Cuvier, 1829)

It is found throughout sub- Saharan Africa, with a preference for permanent fresh water habitats bordered by dense vegetation, such as marshes, reed beds, and estuary (thogh sightings have been recorded in hilly areas with little or no aquatic wildlife presence). The Marsh Mongoose is an important member of the community of animals inhabiting the Papyrus swamps, where deoxygenated water limits aquatic life to various air breathing fish, frogs, insect larvae, snails, and mammals.

1. Physical characteristics

The Marsh Mongoose's dark brown fur (lighter on the undersides), with black-tipped guard hairs, is long and coarse on the body and short about the hands and feet. The paws, underbid with underdeveloped pads, are soft and sensitive, resembling those of a raccoon, with the thumb passively enhancing grip on slippery surfaces. The claws are short and blunt and used for digging. There is little hair around the anus and on the upper lip. Typically, there are two pairs of mammal. The lower canines are well formed while the premolar teeth are thick and used for crushing hard foods. The thick tail narrows shortly to a point.

2. Behaviour

The Marsh Mangoose is a voracious carnivore, consuming any form of meat it can catch, as well as a wide variety of fruit. This mongoose will frequently swim along with river banks, its head above the water, patiently and methodically sifting through underwater holes and crevices looking for aquatic animals to eat. An intelligent creature, the Marsh Mongoose has been observed throwing crabs and snails against rocks in order to break open the shells. The Marsh Mongoose is solitary; spend most living time at night, and crepuscular, though activity has been observed during the day. It is also an excellent swimmer.

Nilgiri Leaf Monkey

Scientific classification

Kingdom	:	Animalia
Phylum	:	Chordata
Class	:	Mammalia
Order	:	Primates
Family	:	Cercopithecidae
Genus	:	Trachypithecus
Species	:	T.johnii

Binomial name

Trachypithecus johnii (J.Fisher, 1829)

Also known as: hooded leaf monkey, Indian hooded leaf monkey, john's langur, Nilgiri black langur, black leaf monkey and Nilgiri leaf monkey.

Vital Statistics

Range	:	India (Western Ghats)
Weight	:	9.8 – 13.6 Kg
Length (Head & Body)	:	49 – 71 Cm
Tail length	:	69 – 97 Cm
Diet	:	Fruits, flowers, seeds
Social unit	:	Troops 8 – 15
Stratum	:	Terrestrial, Arboreal

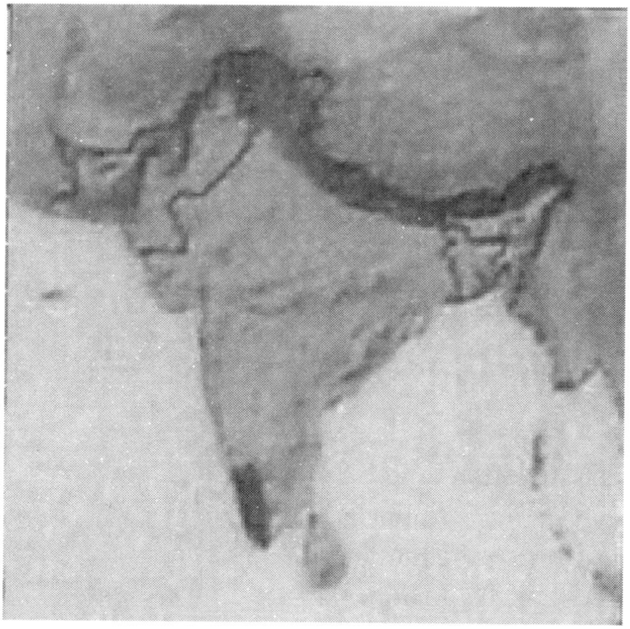

1. Physical characteristics

The Nilgiri Languor has a glossy, dark brown coat and long, thick golden to brown fur on the head. The rump and the start of the tail are highlighted with white, and females have white areas on their inner thighs, obvious from a week old. At birth, the young have pale pink skin and dark red fur, with full adult colouration being attained at three months.

2. Habitat & Ecology

Inhabitats tropical wet evergreen, semi-evergreen and riparian forests as well as teak plantations, at altitudes of between 300- 2,000 m above sea level. Very little is known of the biology of the Nilgiry languor. Young are born mainly in May and November. This languor species form groups with one male and up to 23 female and young, who move through the forest eating the leaves as well as some of their fruit, flowers and seeds. As sub-adults, males begin to fight for access to females, but are then displaced by the dominant male and forced to migrate in all-male groups.

3. Threats

In the past, the Nilgiri langur has suffered from habitat loss and degradation as result of agricultural expansion, mining operations, and dam construction. Currently, habitat loss due to increasing human settlements and deliberate fires, as well as hunting, road kills, and local trade for food, pets and traditional medicine, are the major threats. Locally it is believed that certain parts of the Nilgiri languor's body have medicinal value. The flesh and glands are used to treat asthma and the blood is drunk fresh as a rejuvenator.

4. Conservation

The Nilgiri languor is found in many wildlife sanctuaries in southwestern India. The Wildlife Institute of India suggests that it should be obligatory for the government to restore degraded forests, including the cardamom plantations that have been abandoned following the expiration of the lease. Regular patrolling of forest is necessary to enforce protection of the Nilgiri languor.

Asiatic Black Bear

Scientific classification

Kingdom	:	Animalia
Phylum	:	Chordata
Class	:	Mammalia
Order	:	Carnivora
Family	:	Ursidae
Genus	:	Ursus
Species	:	U. thibetanus

Binomial name

Ursus thibetanus (G. (Baron) Cuvier,1823)

Vital Statistics

Range	:	Asian Continent
Weight	:	
Male	:	110 - 150 Kg
Female	:	60 - 90 Kg
Body Length	:	130 - 190 Cm
Mating Season	:	Spring Season
Diet	:	Grasses, Nuts, invertebrates, small fishes, Honey
Life Span	:	25 years

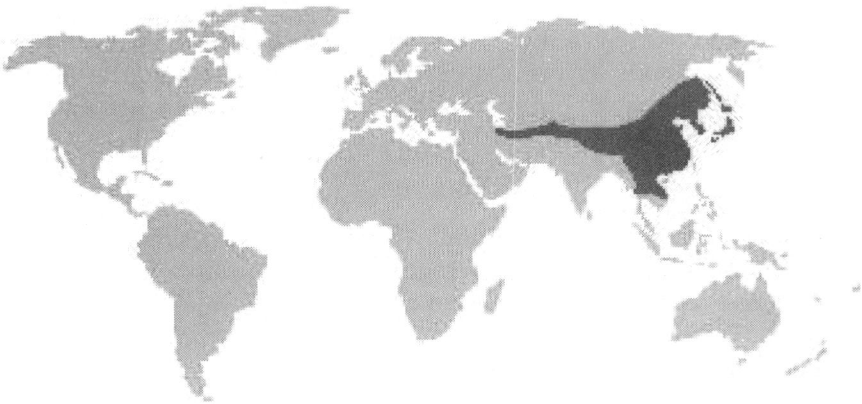

1. Physical characteristics

The Asiatic black bear (Ursus thibetanus or Selenarctos thibetanus), also known as the Tibetan black bear, the Himalayan black bear, or the moon bear, is a medium sized, sharp-clawed, black-coloured bear with a distinctive white or cream 'V' marking on its chest. It is a close relative of the American black bear with which it is thought to share a European common ancestor. The Asiatic black bear grows to approximately 130 to 190 cm (4 ¼ to 6 ¼ ft) in length. Males weigh between 110 and 150 kg (240 to 330 lb) and females weigh between

65 to 90 kg (140 to 200 lb). The bear's life span is around 25 years. It can be found in areas with elevations as high as 4,700 m (13,776 feet), but in lower lands as well. In some parts of its range, the Asiatic black bear shares its habitat with the larger and stronger brown bear.(Ursus arctos)

2. Diet

The Asiatic Black bear is an omnivore which consumes a great variety of foods including fruit, berries, grasses, seeds, nuts, invertebrates, honey and meat (fish, birds, rodents and other small mammals as well as carcasses).

3. Behaviour

The bear ahs been known to be quite aggressive towards human beings(more so than the American black bear); there have been numerous records of bear attacks and killings. This is probably mainly due to the fact that the Asiatic Black bear is more likely to come into contact with people.

4. Status

The Asiatic Black bear has listed as vulnerable on the World Conservation Union's (IUCN) Red List of Threatened Animals. It is threatened mainly by deforestation and habitat loss. The bears are also killed by farmers due to the threat they pose to livestock, and they are also unpopular for their habit of stripping bark from valuable timber trees. Asiatic Black Bears are also threatened by hunting, especially for their gall bladders to obtain bile, which is used in traditional Chinese Medicine.

Indian Elephant

Scientific classification

Kingdom	:	Animalia
Phylum	:	Chordata
Class	:	Mammalia
Order	:	Proboscidea
Family	:	Elephantidae
Genus	:	Elephas
Species	:	E. maximus
Subspecies	:	E.m.indicus

Bionomial name

Elephas maximus indicus (Linnaeus,1775)

Vital Statistics

Range	:	India, Nepal, Bhutan, Bangladesh, Myanmar
Weight	:	3.5 tones
Shoulder Height	:	6.6 – 11 feet
Sexual Maturity	:	Around 20 years
Gestation Period	:	22 Months
Young per birth	:	1 - 2
Diet	:	Grasses, leaves, fruits
Life Span	:	70 years
Social Unit	:	Family / Solitary Male
Conservation Threats	:	Poaching, habitat loss and human animal conflict

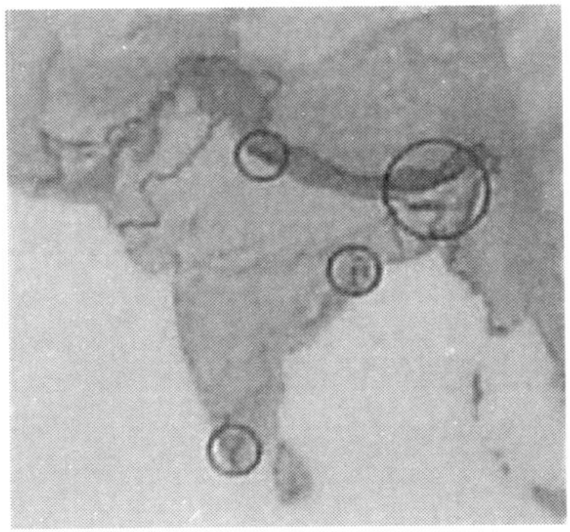

1. Distribution

The Indian Elephant is found in the wild in densely forested areas of India including the tropical forests of South India, North East India and the sub Himalayan region. Also known as the Asian Elephant it is found in Sri Lanka, Bangladesh, Bhutan, Nepal, Thailand, Malaysia, Myanmar, Viet Nam, Cambodia, Indonesia, Laos and China.

2. Anatomy

Elephants are the largest of all mammals on land. The Indian Elephant is smaller than the African Elephant, however it can grow up to 11 feet tall and weigh up to 5 tons. The elephant's brain is the heaviest of all land mammals and can weigh up to 5 kg. Elephants have large ears, are covered with grey hairy skin, and characterized by their long trunks which can be used in a number of ways for breathing, to suck in water or food, to lift and pull objects, and to make trumpeting noises and other sounds for communication. All male Indian Elephants do not have tusks. Elephants that do have large tusks are hunted by poachers who seek the tusks for their ivory. The tusks, which are elongated incisor teeth, are used for digging, pushing and fighting with other male elephants. The molar teeth which elephants use for chewing are located within their mouths and are replaced as they get worn out, until about age 40.

3. Diet

Elephants are herbivorous creatures and spend a large amount of time everyday eating upto 300 kg of vegetation, including grass, leaves, fruit and the bark of trees. The length of an elephant's digestive system is around 100 feet. Elephants that are tamed are fed on leaves, sugarcane, bananas and rice gruel.

4. Behaviour

Elephants have a complex social structure. In the wild they live in family groups led by mature female elephants, their young and sometimes older bull elephants. Mature male elephants are often solitary or live in small groups of male elephants only. Elephants live up to 70 years old and can sleep while standing. Tame elephants are made to sit or lie down while its trainer or mahout attends to it, in the wild, however, elephant will not lie down unless it is sick.

Elephants enjoy wallowing in water, which helps clean their skin, which does not have sweat glands. Adult male elephants around the age of 20 undergo a phase of heightened sexual urge known as "musth." Male elephants become aggressive and violent for a phase lasting up to 60 days. This phase recurs periodically through an adult male elephant's life. Female elephants can bear young around the age of 16. Usually one, but sometimes two, offspring are born at a time. Elephants give birth to about 4 young ones over a span of 60 years. Elephants communicate through a variety of noises, including infrasonic sounds, which are inaudible to human beings.

5. Status

Indian Elephants are threatened by poaching for their tusks, by the loss of habitat due to human pressure on forest areas and due to human conflict. The isolated populations of wild elephants in individual wildlife sanctuaries are also threatened by loss of genetic diversity. Recently a number of corridors connecting wildlife sanctuaries have been established to encourage the migration of wild elephants.

Wild Asian Water Buffalo

Scientific classification

Kingdom	:	Animalia
Phylum	:	Chordata
Class	:	Mammalia
Order	:	Artiodactyla
Family	:	Bovidae
Subfamily	:	Bovinae
Tribe	:	Bovini
Genus	:	Bubalus
Species	:	B. bubalis (B. arnee)

Binomial name

Bubalus bubalis (B. arnee) (Linnaeus, 1758)

Vital Statistics

Size	:	5ft. 6 in
Weight		
Male	:	1200 Kg
Female	:	900 Kg
Horn Measurement	:	77 $^3/_8$ inches
Distribution	:	Brahmaputra in Assam, Orissa, Madhya Pradesh

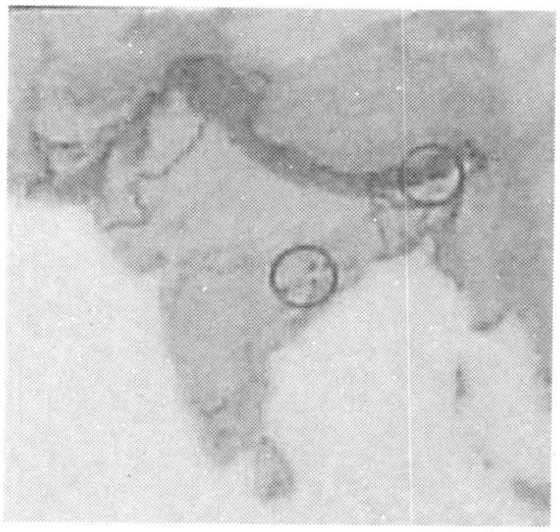

True Wild Asian Water Buffalo or Wild Asiatic Water Buffalo is an endangered species. It is thought to survive in Bangladesh, India, Nepal, Bhutan and Thailand. It is a large ungulate and a member of the bovine subfamily

Physical characteristics

In the wild, wild Asian water buffalo can weigh up to 800 to 900 Kg for females, and males, 1200 kg. They can stand as tall as 1.8m at the shoulder, and stretch up to 2.9m in body length. However, the wild buffalo subspecies found in the Assam state of Northern India, where they inhabit monsoon forests along the foothills of the Himalaya, are notably larger. Here, the average weight of a wild adult buffalo is 900 kg, with the male considerably larger than the female. The average height at the shoulder for a male is about 1.7m, and may reach even 2 metres.

Distinctive Characters

Though it has a finer carriage the Wild Buffalo differs little in general appearance from the tame one, except perhaps that it is sleeker, heavier, and more robust-looking. Like the domestic buffalo, the Wild Buffalo is a slaty black. The legs are dirty white upto just above the hocks and the knees. The newborn calf is light coloured, almost yellow. As to horns, Wild Buffalo usually exhibit two types. In one, the horns curve upwards in a semicircle, the tips being. separated by a small interval. In the second, the horns spread outwards almost horizontally from the head and curve slightly upwards and inwards near the tips. Both types may be found in the same herd and there is much intergrading between the two forms. The horns are fiat and triangular in section; those of the cows are less massive and vary less in shape.

Distribution

The grass jungles of the Nepal Terai and the plains of the Brahmaputra in Assam; a few herds survive in parts of Orissa adjoining Bastar District of Madhya Pradesh

Habits

Tall grass jungles and reed brakes in the neighbourhood of swamps provide the ideal habitat for buffaloes, offering them both food and shelter, pools of water to lie in, and mud wallows in which to roll and cake themselves with earth. Such is their habitat in the riverain flats of Assam and the Terai. In the southern parts of their range they live on drier harder ground, well broken up into nullahs and scattered with trees and open expanses of grass. They associate in small herds which may combine to form large assemblages.

Threat

Wild Asian Water Buffalo are threatened by genetic pollution when they come into contact with common abundant Domestic Asian Water Buffalo which live in and around forests. The domesticated animals daily graze within forests which have been designated as wildlife sanctuaries and national parks for their wild ancestors.

VULNERABLE

Asiatic Wild Ass

Scientific classification

Kingdom	:	Animalia
Phylum	:	Chordata
Class	:	Mammalia
Order	:	Perissodactyla
Family	:	Equidae
Genus	:	Equus
Subgenus	:	Asinus
Species	:	E. hemionus

Binomial name

Equus hemionus (Pallas, 1775)

Vital Statistics

Range	:	India, Pakistan, Iran, Tibet
Weight	:	290 Kg
Body Length	:	210 Cm
Tail Length	:	50 Cm
Shoulder Height	:	140 Cm
Sexual Maturity	:	After 1 year
Gestation Period	:	12 Months
Young per birth	:	1
Diet	:	Grasses
Life Span	:	20 years
Distribution	:	The desert of the Rann of cutch

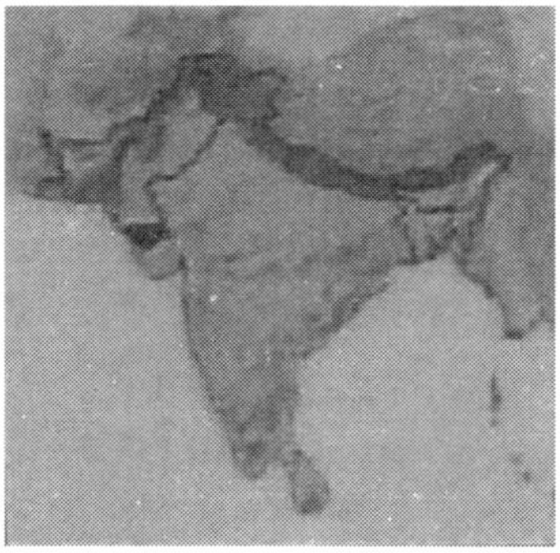

The Onager (Equus hemionus) is a large mammal belonging to the horse family and native to the deserts of Syria, Iran, Pakistan, India, Israel, and Tibet. It is sometimes known as the Asian Wild Ass.

1. Physical characteristics

Onagers are a little larger than donkeys at about 290 kg and 2.1 meters (head-body length), and are a little more horse-like. They are short-legged compared to horses, and their coloring varies depending on the season. They are generally reddish-brown in color during the summer, becoming yellowish-brown in the winter months. They have a black stripe bordered in white that extends down the middle of the back. They are notoriously untamable.

2. Distinctive Characters

The general color of its coat various from reddish grey to fawn or pale chestnut. They erect dark brown mane is continue as a dark brown stripe extending along the back to the root of the tail; lower parts, white.

3. Habits

They are attracted by the flat grass - covered expanses known as bets. These bets form Islands are oases of coarse grasses which spring of vigorously with monsoon inundation

4. Threats

Like many other large grazing animals, its range has contracted greatly under the pressures of hunting and habitat loss, and of the six subspecies, one is extinct and two endangered. The Kiang (E.Kiang), a Tibetan relative, was previously considered to be a subspecies of the Onager as E.hemionus kiang, but recent molecular studies indicate that its a distinct species.

Nilgiri Marten

Scientific classification

Kingdom	:	Animalia
Phylum	:	Chordata
Class	:	Mammalia
Order	:	Carnivora
Family	:	Mustelidae
Genus	:	Martes
Species	:	M.gwatkinsii

Binomial name

Martes gwatkinsii (Horsfield, 1851)

The Nilgiri Marten (Martes gwatkinsii) is the only species of marten found in southern India. It occurs in the hills of the Nilgiris and parts of the Western Ghats.

1. Physical characteristics

The Nilgiri Marten is similar to the yellow-throated marten, but is larger and essentially different in the structure of the skull - it has a prominent frontal concavity. It is unmistakable in the field as it is dark above with a bright throat ranging in colour from yellow to orange. It is about 55 to 65 cm along from head to vent and has a tail of 40 to 45 cm. It weighs about 2.1 kg.

2. Ecology and behaviour

Very little is known about the Nilgiri Marten. It is diurnal, and though arboreal descends to the ground occasionally. It is reported to prey on birds, small mammals and insects such as Cicadas.

Nonsense Rat

Scientific classification

Kingdom	:	Animalia
Phylum	:	Chordata
Class	:	Mammalia
Order	:	Rotentia
Family	:	Muridae
Subfamily	:	Murinae
Genus	:	Rattus
Species	:	R.burrus

Binomial name

Rattus burrus (Miller, 1902)

Common Name	:	Miller's rat
Occurrence	:	Endemic to Little and reta Nicobars and Trinker Islands
Identification	:	Similar to Malaysian Wood rat
Diet	:	Seeds, grass
Social groups	:	2 – 3
Activity	:	Nocturnal
Stratum	:	Terrestrial, fossorial
Common threats	:	Pesticides, Human interfernce

The Nonsense Rat, Rattus burrus, is currently listed as a vulnerable species (2003), and this particular species of rat is also endemic to India. The Nonsense Rat was first reported in 1902 by Miller.

Palm Rat

Scientific classification

Kingdom	:	Animalia
Phylum	:	Chordata
Class	:	Mammalia
Order	:	Rotentia
Family	:	Muridae
Genus	:	Rattus
Species group	:	R.rattus
Species	:	R.palmarum

Binomial name

Rattus palmarum (Zelebor, 1869)

Vital Statistics

Common Name	:	Nicobar rat
Occurrence	:	Endemic to Nicobar Islands
Identification	:	Very large rat around 27.5 cm Under sides are pale grey
Tail	:	Two – thirds of body size
Diet	:	Seeds, grass
Social groups	:	2 – 3
Activity	:	Nocturnal
Stratum	:	Terrestrial, fossorial
Common threats	:	Pesticides, Human interfernce

The Palm Rat (Rattus palmarum) is a species of rodent in the Muridae family. It is found only in India. Its natural habitats are subtropical or tropical dry forests and subtropical or tropical mangrove forests.

Takin

Scientific classification

Kingdom	:	Animalia
Phylum	:	Chordata
Class	:	Mammalia
Order	:	Artiodactyla
Family	:	Bovidae
Subfamily	:	Caprinae
Genus	:	Budorcas
Species	:	B.taxicolor

Binomial name

Budorcas taxicolor (Hodgson, 1850)

Vital Statistics

Range	: India
Weight	: 350 Kg
Shoulder Height	: 110 - 120 Cm
Horn Length	: 30Cm
Diet	: Grasses, buds, leaves
Conservation Threats	: Poaching
Best Seen	: At Jorging Valley, Siang (Arunachala Pradesh)

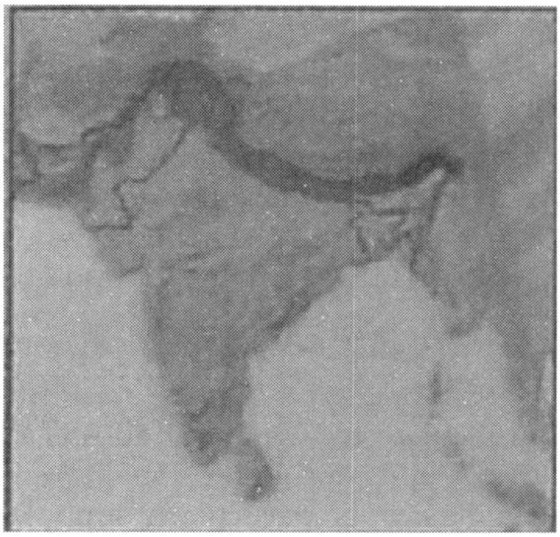

The Takin (Budorcas taxicolor) is a goat-antelope found in heavily forested areas of the Eastern Himalayas. There are four subspecies: B.taxicolour, the Mishmi Takin; B.taxicolour bedfordi, the Shensi or Golden Takin; B.taxicolor tibetana, the Tibetan or Sichuan Takin; and B.taxocolour whitei, the Bhutan Takin. The takin is the national animal of Bhutan.

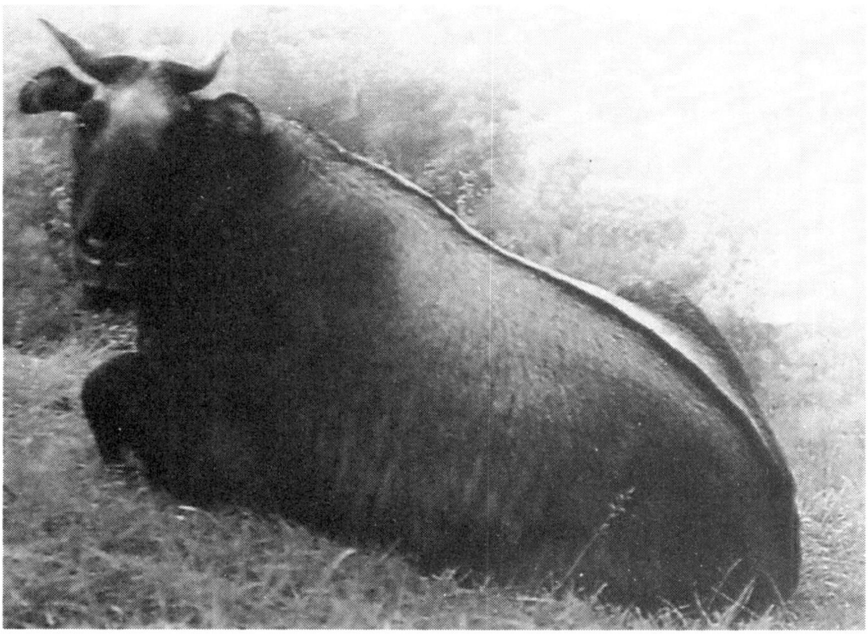

1. Physical Characteristics

Takin's stand 110 to 120 centimetres (3 to 4 feet) at the shoulder and weigh up to 350 kg. Takin's have large muscles and eyes with noticeably small ears. They are sometimes referred to as "beestung moose". They are covered in a thick golden wool which turns black on the under-belly. Both sexes have small horns which run parallel to the skull and then turn upwards in a short point, these are around 30 centimeters long.

2. Diet and Behaviour

Takin are found in Bamboo forests at altitudes 0f 2,000 4,500 metres - where they eat grass, buds and leaves. Takin,s are dinurnal, active in the day, resting in the heat on particularly sunny days. Takin gather in small herds in winter and herds of upto a hundred individuals in the summer, old males are solitary. The Takin is attracted to hot sulphur springs where it gathers in large numbers. Its body is covered by an oily substance with a characteristic odour.

Himalayan Crestless Porcupine

Scientific classification

Kingdom	:	Animalia
Phylum	:	Chordata
Class	:	Mammalia
Order	:	Rotentia
Family	:	Hystricidae
Genus	:	Hystrix
Species	:	H. brachyura

Binomial name

Hystrix brachyuran (Linnaeus, 1758)

Vital Statistics

Range	:	India, China, Indonesia, Myanmar
Body Length	:	60 – 90 Cm
Tail Length	:	20 – 25 Cm
Height Body Length	:	45 – 75 cm
Quills Length	:	75 mm
Weight	:	5 – 8 Kg
Social Unit	:	Solitary / groups of 2 – 4
Stratum	:	Fossorial, terrestrial
Diet	:	Roots, grains, fruits
Best Seen	:	At Orang NP (Assam)
Conservation Threats	:	Habitat loss and poaching
Habitats and occurrence	:	Forests and grasslands of eastern Himalaya, especially in and around cultivated land

The Himalayan Crestless Porcupine (**Hystrix brachyura**) is a species of rodent in the Hystricidae family. It is found in Cambodia, China, India, Indonesia, Laos, Malaysia, Myanmar,Nepal, Singapore, Thailand and Vietnam.

A large, stocky rodent with a short tail and a very short or rudimentary dorsal crest, the Crestless Porcupine is also called the Hodgson's Porcupine. This is the common porcupine of Northeast India. It can be distinguished from the Indian Porcupine by its shorter dorsal crest (15 cm instead of up to 30 cm).

1. Physical Characteristics

Porcupines are about 25-36 inches (60-90 cm) long, with an 8-10 inch (20-25 cm) long tail. Weighing between 12-35 pounds (5-16 kg), they are rounded, large and slow. Porcupines come in various shades of brown, grey, and the unusual white. The animal's quills or spines take on various forms, depending on the species, but all are modified hairs coated with thick plates of Keratin, and they are embedded in the skin musculature. Old World Porcupines (Hystricidae) have quills embedded in clusters, whereas in New World Porcupines (Erethizontidae) single quills are interspersed with bristles, under fur, and hair.

New World Porcupines

New World porcupines are mostly smaller, their quills attached singly rather than grouped in clusters, and are excellent climbers, spending much of their time in trees. The New World Porcupines evolved their spines independently convergent evolution) and are more closely related to several other families of rodent than they are to the Old World porcupines.

Sloth Bear

Scientific classification

Kingdom	:	Animalia
Phylum	:	Chordata
Class	:	Mammalia
Order	:	Carnivora
Family	:	Ursidae
Genus	:	Melursus
Species	:	M.Ursinus

Binomial name

Melursus ursinus (Shaw, 1791)

Vital Statistics

Range	:	India, Nepal, Bhutan, Bangladesh, Srilanka
Weight		
Male	:	80 – 140 Kg
Female	:	55 – 95 Kg
Body Length	:	150 - 190 Cm
Mating Season	:	May, June, July
Gestation Period	:	7 Months
Young per birth	:	2 - 3
Diet	:	Ants, Termites, eggs, honey, fruits

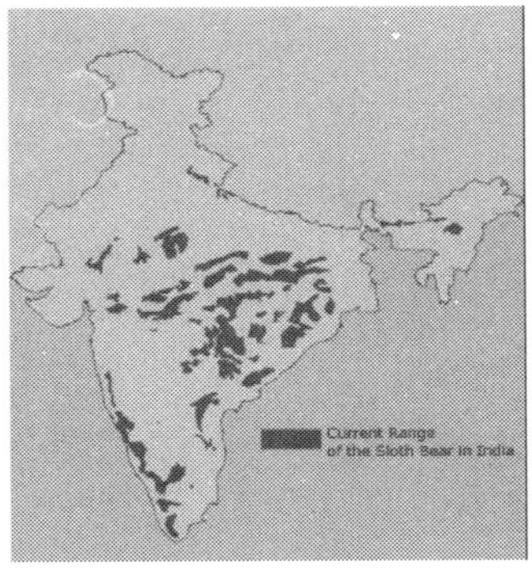

The Sloth Bear (Melursus ursinus) is a nocturnal bear, inhabiting the lowland forests of India, Nepal, Bhutan, Bangladesh and Sri Lanka. The Sloth Bear is the only bear species classified in genus Melursus.

1. Physical characteristics

The body is 150 – 190 cm long, covered in long, shaggy fur, ranging from auburn to black, with a distinctive "V" shaped white mark on the chest, a whitish snout and black nose. The snout is long with bare lips and a lack of upper incisors, adaptations for its insect based diet. The front feet are turned inwards and have not-retractable, curved ivory claws that are adapted for digging. The males, weighing 80-140 kg, are larger than the females, which weigh only 55-95 kg. Its pugmarks are very similar to a human footprint.

2. Diet

The Sloth Bear primarily eats ants and termites, breaking into termite mounds with large powerful claws and eating the occupants. It may also eat honey, eggs, birds, flowers, tubers, fruits, grains and meat.

The animal's fondness for honey has caused it to be nicknamed the **Honey bear**.

3. Conservation

Poaching and loss of the habitat and fragmentation of available habitat are the primary threats to the survival of the Sloth Bear on the Indian Subcontinent. Predators such as the Leopard, wolves and the Tiger may attempt to prey on the young, though the female Sloth Bear with young is exceptionally vicious regarding any threats to her young. Adults defend themselves quite well with their claws. Humans hunt the Sloth Bear primarily for its gall bladder, which is valued in eastern medicine. The Sloth Bear's current conservation status is vulnerable.

Himalayan Musk Deer

Scientific classification

Kingdom	:	Animalia
Phylum	:	Chordata
Class	:	Mammalia
Order	:	Artiodactyla
Family	:	Moschidae
Genus	:	Moschus
Species	:	M. leucogaster

Binomial name

Moschus leucogaster (Hodgson,1839)

Vital Statistics

Range	:	India, Nepal
Weight	:	11 – 18 Kg
Body Length	:	86 - 100 Cm
Tail Length	:	4 – 6 Cm
Shoulder Height	:	51 – 53 Cm
Sexual Maturity	:	16 – 24 Months
Gestation Period	:	185 – 195 days
Young per birth	:	1 - 2
Diet	:	Leaves, grasses, Moss, lichens, shoots, twigs
Life Span	:	12 – 20 years

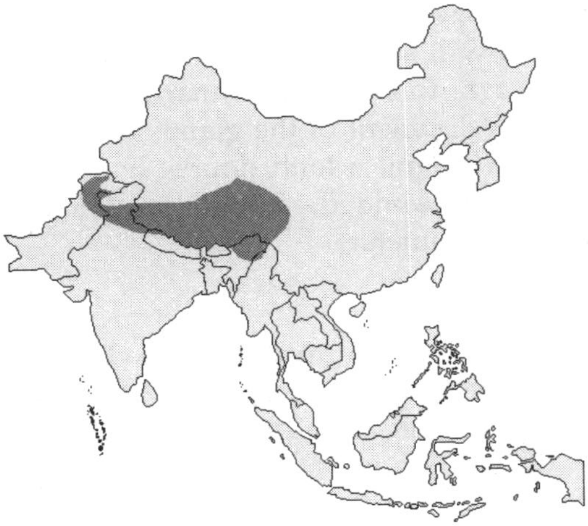

1. Distribution

Alpine forest and scrub at elevations of 2,200-4,300 meters/ 7250-14,200 feet on the eastern and southern edge of Tibet and the southern slopes of the Himalayas.

2. Physical characteristics

The general colour of the coat, composed of brittle hairs, is a slightly grizzled sandy brown. As the name suggests, on the chest is a wide vertical whitish-yellow stripe which extends up the throat to the chin. The ears are tipped with yellow or orange hairs. On the nape of the neck are several horizontal blotches of yellowish hairs. The body slopes forward, as the hind legs are almost one third longer than the forelegs, causing the weight at the rump to be almost 10 cm / 4 inches above the shoulder. The ears are large and rounded, generally lined with whitish fur. Both sexes have well-developed upper canines, and in males these grow 7-10 cm / 3-4 inches long and protrude from the mouth in a fang-like manner. The canines are constantly growing, but, due to their mobility and fragility, they are easily broken. There are no antlers in this, as well as other musk deer, species.

3. Ecology and Behaviour

Himalayan musk deer are most active between dusk and dawn, alternately resting and feeding throughout this period. At night, musk deer can be seen in the open areas of their habitat as they graze, while during the day, they remain in the dense cover. Neighbouring individuals may utilize common latrines, an activity with becomes more frequent during the mating season.

Drastic changes in direction are made during flight, and every few jumps the animal will stop and listen. Communication between individuals is thought to be based primarily on their sense of smell, due to the high development of the glands of musk deer. Primarily silent, musk deer will emit a loud double hiss if alarmed, and may scream plaintively if wounded. Population densities are about 3-4 animals per square kilometer.

4. Conservation Status

As a species, the Himalayan musk deer is classified as a low risk, near threatened by the IUCN (1996). M.c. chrysogaster and M.c.leucogaster are both classified as low risk, near threatened subspecies.

Indian Giant Squirrel

Scientific classification

Kingdom	:	Animalia
Phylum	:	Chordata
Class	:	Mammalia
Order	:	Rotentia
Family	:	Sciuridae
Genus	:	Ratufa
Species	:	R. indica

Binomial name

Ratufa indica (Erxleben, 1777)

Vital Statistics

Range	:	South East Asia
Weight	:	2 Kg
Body Length	:	36 – 41 Cm
Tail Length	:	2 feet
Diet	:	fruits

1. Distribution

The Indian giant squirrel, Ratufa indica, is a large-bodied diurnal, arboreal, and herbivorous squirrel found in South Asia. Also called the Malabar giant squirrel, the species is endemic to deciduous, mixed deciduous, and moist evergreen forests of peninsular India , reaching as far north as the Satpura hill range of Madhya Pradesh.

2. Morphology

The Ratufa indica has a conspicuous bipartite(and sometimes tripartite) colouring pattern. The colours involved can be creamy-beige, buff, tan,rust, brown or even a dark seal brown. The underparts and the front legs are usually cream coloured, the head can be brown or beige, however there is a distinctive white spot between the ears. Seven different geographical races, each distinctive in the colouration of its upper-parts, have been identified. Among these are the buff and tan Ratufa indica dealbata of the tropical moist deciduous forests of the Surat Dangs; the seal brown, tan and beige (and darkest) Ratufa indica maxima of the tropical wet evergreen forest of Malabar; the dark brown, tan and beige(and largest), Ratufa indica bengalensis of the tropical semi-evergreen forests each of the Brahmagiri mountains in Coorg extending up to the Bay of Bengal coast of Orissa; and the rust and buff Ratufa indica centralis of the tropical dry deciduous forests of Central India, near Hoshangabad

3. Physical characteristics

Adult head and body length varies between 14-16 in (36-41 cm) and the tail length is approximately 2 ft (0.61 m). Adult weight is 2 kg(4.41 lb).

4. Behaviour

It often sleeps draped over a branch, with its tail falling over.

5. Habitat and Occurrence

Mixed deciduous and evergreen forests south of 22°N.

Brown Bear

Scientific classification

Kingdom	:	Animalia
Phylum	:	Chordata
Class	:	Mammalia
Order	:	Carnivora
Family	:	Ursidae
Genus	:	Ursus
Species	:	U.arctos

Binomial name

Ursus arctos (Linnaeus, 1758)

Vital Statistics

Range	:	Asia
Weight	:	130 - 700 Kg
Head and Body Length	:	245 cm
Shoulder Height	:	90 – 150 Cm
Young per birth	:	1 - 4
Diet	:	Plants, fishes, insects
Conservation Thread	:	Habitat disturbance and poaching
Best Seen	:	At Great Himalayan NP (Himachal Pradesh

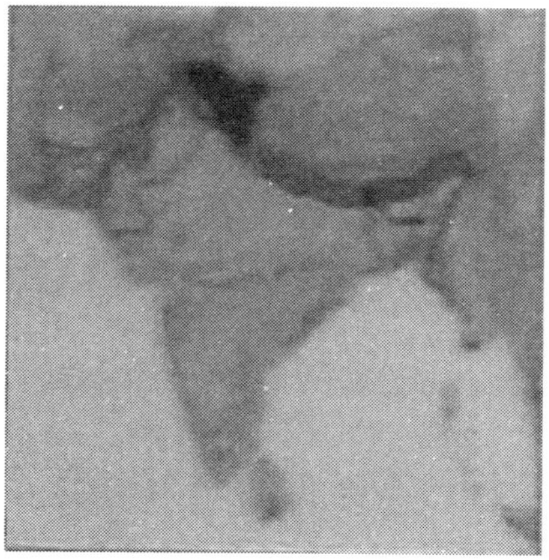

1. Morphology

Brown bears have furry coats in shades of blonde, brown, black or a combination of those colors. The longer outer guard hairs of the brown bear are often tipped with white or silver, giving a "grizzled" appearance. They have a very short, stubby tail, just like all bears in the world. Brown bears have a large hump of muscle over their shoulders, which give strength to the forelimbs for digging.

2. Physical Characteristics

Forearms end in massive paws with very powerful claws up to 15 cm in length. Their heads are large and round with a concave facial profile. The normal range of physical dimensions for a brown bear is a head-and-body length of 1.7 to 2.8 m (5.6 to 9.2 feet) and a shoulder height 90 to 150 cm(35 to 59 inches), although the abnormally large specimens exceed this measurement.

3. Diet

They are omnivores and feed on a variety of plant parts, including berries, roots and sprouts, fungi, fish, insects and small mammals, especially ground squirrels. Despite their reputation, most brown bears are not particularly carnivorous as they derive up to 90% of their dietary food energy from vegetable matter. Brown bears also occasionally prey on deer, red deer, moose and bison. When brown bears attack these animals, they tend to choose the young ones since they are much easier to catch. They also feed on carrion and will drive wolves, cougars, black bears and Siberian tigers from their kills.

4. Behaviour

In spite of their size, some have been clocked at speeds in excess of 56 km/h (35 mph). Along with their strength and deceptive speed, brown bears are legendary for their stamina. They are capable of running at full speed for miles at a time without stopping.

The brown bear is primarily nocturnal and, in the summer, puts on up to 180 kg (400 pounds) of fat, on which it relies to make it through winter, when it becomes very lethargic. Although they are not full hibernators, and can be woken easily, both sexes like to den in a protected spot such as a cave, crevice or hollow log during the winter months.

Normally a solitary animal, the brown bear congregates alongside streams and rivers during the salmon spawn in the fall. In alternate years, females produce one to four young, which weigh only about 1 to 2 kg (2 to 5 lb) at birth. Raised entirely by their mother, cubs climb trees when in danger.

6. Threats

Attacks usually occur because the bear is injured or a human encounters a mother bear with cubs.

Slow Loris

Scientific classification

Kingdom	:	Animalia
Phylum	:	Chordata
Class	:	Mammalia
Order	:	Primates
Family	:	Lorisidae
Subfamily	:	Lorinae
Genus	:	Nycticebus bengalensis

Bionomial name

(E. Geoffroy, 1812)

Vital Statistics

Range	:	South East Asia
Weight	:	2 Kg
Length	:	31 – 38 Cm
Gestation Period	:	190 days
Young per birth	:	1, rarely 2
Diet	:	Insects, small vertebrates
Life span	:	14 years
Social Unit	:	Solitary / Pairs
Conservation Threads	:	Poaching and habitat loss
Best Seen	:	At Panbari and Kanchanjuri, Kaziranga NP (Assam)

1. Physical Characteristics

Adult slow lorises range in size from 21 to 38 cm, depending on the species and weigh up to 2 kliograms. The tail is a mere stump. The

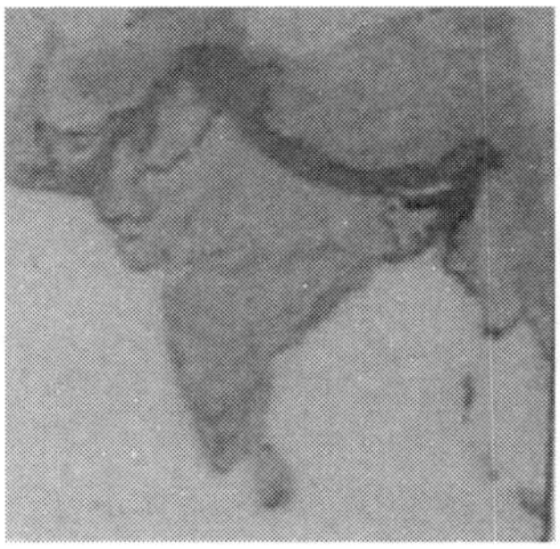

short, thick fur can have a variety of color, mostly grey-reddish and often with whitish undertones. They have well developed thumbs, which they use to grasp and hold fast to branches, and a very flexible back. The eyes are large and point forward, and the ears are small and nearly hidden in the fur. They are generally more strongly built than the slender lorises.

2. Diet

Slow lorises are opportunistic carnivores, typically eating insects, bird eggs and small vertebrates. With their slow quiet movements, they creep to their prey, in order to catch it with a lightning – quick snatch. They also eat fruits, but rarely.

3. Behaviour

Like all lorises, slow lorises are nocturnal and arboreal animals that prefer the tops of the trees. Also, they have slow, deliberate movements and a powerful grasp that makes them difficult to remove from branches. They live as solitaries or in small family groups, and mark their territory with urine.

Clouded Leopard

Scientific classification

Kingdom	:	Animalia
Phylum	:	Chordata
Class	:	Mammalia
Order	:	Carnivora
Family	:	Felidae
Subfamily	:	Pantherinae
Genus	:	Neofelis
Species	:	N.nebulosa

Binomial name

Neofelis nebulosa (Griffith, 1821)

Vital Statistics

Range	:	India, China, South East Asia
Length	:	55 – 110 Cm
Weight	:	15 - 23 Kg
Sexual Maturity	:	2 years
Gestation Period	:	85 – 93 days
Young per birth	:	1 - 5
Diet	:	Sambar Dear, Civiet, Pigs, Monkeys
Life Span	:	17 years

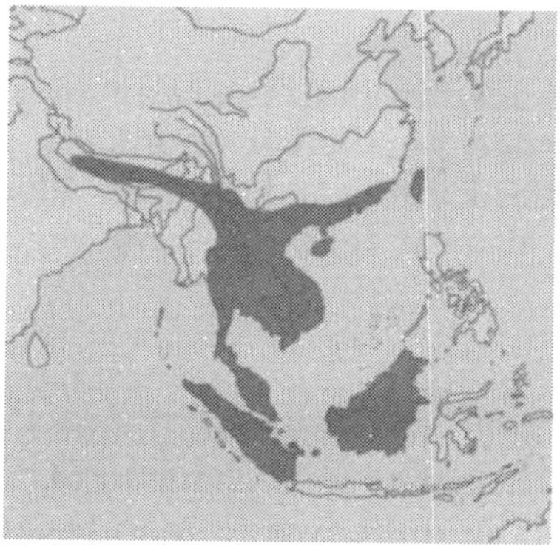

1. Physical Characteristics

The Clouded Leopard(Neofelis nebulosa) is a medium-sized cat, 55 to 110 cm (2 ft to 3 ft 6 in) long and weighing between 15 and 23 kg (33 to 50 lb). It has a tan or tawny coat, and is distinctively marked with large, irregularly-shaped, dark-edged ellipses which are said to be shaped like clouds, hence both its common and original scientific name. The Clouded Leopard has 5 toes like most big cats. The Clouded Leopard is an excellent climber. Short, flexible legs, large paws, and keen claws combine to make it very surefooted. The Clouded Leopard can possess a tail as long as its body, further aiding in balance. Surprisingly, the cat can climb while hanging upside-down under branches and descend tree trunks head-first.

2. Habitat

It ranges through southern China, the eastern Himalayas, north-east India, and south-east Asia. Preferred habitat is tropical and subtropical forests at altitudes up to about 2,000 meters (6,500 ft), However it is sometimes found in mangrove swamps and grassland. It lives in temperatures from 65 to 120 degrees.

3. Diet

Like most cats the clouded leopard is a carnivore. Its prey is sambar, muntjac, birds, bearded pigs, civet, monkeys, gibbons, squirrels, porcupines, fish, domestic cattle and chicken. Clouded Leopards that are held in captivity also eat eggs and some vegetation.

4. Behaviour

Little is known about its behaviour in the wild, but it is assumed that it is highly arboreal and their favoured hunting tactic is to drop on prey from the trees. The habits and behaviour of the Clouded Leopard in the wild are virtually unknown to man because of the animal's secretive nature. With a lack of evidence for a pack-or pride-society like that of the Lion, it is assumed that it is a generally solitary creature. Certainly it interacts with other Clouded Leopards while engaged in activities relating to mating and rearing young. While it was once assumed that the Clouded Leopard was active only at night, the cat has now been observed during the day.

5. Conservation and threats

Because the Clouded Leopard's habits make it difficult to study, reliable estimates of its population do not exist. Habitat loss due to widespread deforestation and hunting for use in Chinese medicinal preparations are thought to be causing populations of the Clouded Leopard to decline. CITES, the Convention on International Trade in Endangered species of wild Fauna and Flora, lists Clouded Leopard as an Appendix I species.

Dhole

Scientific classification

Kingdom	:	Animalia
Phylum	:	Chordata
Class	:	Mammalia
Order	:	Carnivora
Family	:	Canidae
Subfamily	:	Caninae
Genus	:	Cuon
Species	:	C. alpinus

Binomial name

Cuon alpinus (Pallas, 1811)

Vital Statistics

Range	:	South Asia
Weight		
Male	:	10 – 16 Kg
Female	:	14 - 22 Kg
Length		
Head & Body	:	88 – 133 Cm
Tail	:	28 – 50 Cm
Shoulder Height	:	42 – 55 Cm
Sexual Maturity	:	15 Months
Mating Season	:	January - March
Gestation Period	:	60 – 62 days
Young per birth	:	8 pups
Diet	:	Spotted Dear, wild boar, hares
Life Span	:	10 years

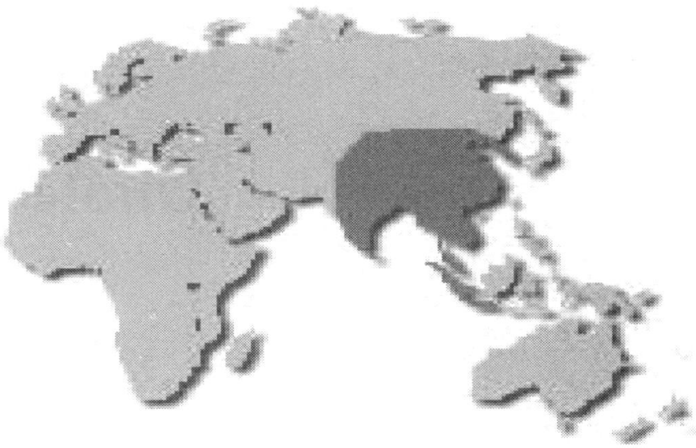

The Dhole (Cuon alpinus) is a species of wild dog of the Canidae family. It is also known as the Asiatic Wild Dog; lesser known names include the Indian Wild Dog, the Red Dog, the Asiatic Dog, and the Whistling Hunter (due to whistling sound it can make).

1. Habitat

The Dholes exploits a large variety of habitats, reflecting its adaptability. It normally inhabits dry and moist deciduous forests and thick jungles, as well as tropical rain forests, which all provide better cover for hunting.

2. Physical Characteristics

The Dholes is about the size of a collie, and is similar to the dingo and golden jackal. Its coat is usually a uniformly rusty red hue, but varies regionally from sandy, creamy yellow through red and brown to dark grey. Sometimes it is grizzled. Generally, the Dholes has a black-tipped-though sometimes white or brown or grey- moderately bushy tail, a darker area on its back, and white or pale patches on its chest, paws and belly. Its large ears (about half the length of the face) are rounded with white on the inside, its legs are short, and its eyes are slightly hooded and have amber irises. The Dhole has sixteen teats, reflecting its ability to care for many young. This is more teats than most other dogs. It has four toes on each paw, with fur between the toes, which are red, brown, and/or white. The fore-toe pads are hairless, and are joined at the base near the main pad, unlike most domestic dogs. The jaw is thick, blunt, relatively short, slightly convex in profile and squarish.

3. Diet

The dhole is an omnivore. Its prey are usually deer(like spotted deer, chital and sambar, the latter of which is over twenty times a dhole's weight), but also wild boar, red muntjac deer, wild goats, wild sheep, nilgai, mountain sheep, water buffalo, hares (like the Black-naped Hare), caribou, reindeer, gaur and sometimes monkeys.

4. Behaviour

Generally it lives in organized, extended-family packs of five to twelve individuals (this number rarely exceeds twenty five), with more males, sometimes twice as many more, than females, and usually just one breeding female. Sometimes pack members interact with other dholes outside of their own group; these interactions may be positive or hostile(home ranges are often quite separate). Environmental conditions can affect group size and composition. Large packs of over forty dholes have been sighted, possibly resulting from the temporary fusion of neighboring packs. Older dholes of around 7-8 years sometimes vanish from the group.

5. Conservation

In India , bounties were paid for carcasses until wide dholes was declared a Protected Species under Schedule 1 of the Wildlife Act of 1972 which prohibits the killing of wildlife except in self-defense; or if the dholes is a man-killer-and, even then, permission is required. Hunting of dholes in the Soviet Union had been prohibited since 1971; they received the status of 'protected animal' I 1974.

Blackbuck

Scientific classification

Kingdom	:	Animalia
Phylum	:	Chordata
Class	:	Mammalia
Order	:	Artiodactyla
Family	:	Bovidae
Subfamily	:	Antilopinae
Genus	:	Antelope Pallas, 1766
Species	:	A.cervicapra

Binomial name

Antilope cervicapra (Linnaeus,1758)

Blackbuck (Antilope cervicapra) is a species of antelope found mainly in India, but also in parts of Pakistan and Nepal.

Vital Statistics

Range	:	India, Pakistan, Nepal
Weight	:	75 – 95 pounds
Height	:	80 Cm
Horn Length	:	70 Cm
Gestation Period	:	150 days
Young per birth	:	1
Diet	:	Grasses, leaves, buds and shoots
Life Span	:	12 – 16 years

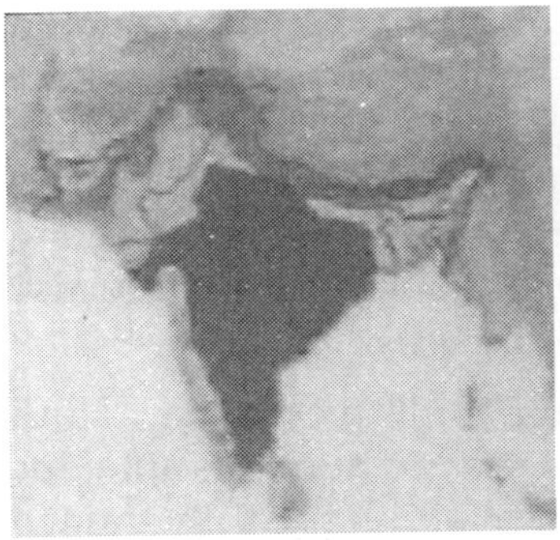

1. Habitat

Originally spread over large tracts of India (except in North East India). Today the Blackbuck population is confined to areas in Punjab, Rajasthan, Haryana and Gujarat with a few small pockets in Central India. Its original habitat is open plain and not dense jungles. One the open plain, the Blackbuck is one of the fastest animals and can outrun most predators over long distances.

2. Physical Characteristics

The horns of the Blackbuck are ringed with 1 to 4 turns, rarely more than 4 turns, and can be as long as 28 inches. A trophy Blackbuck is 18+ inches. In the male, the upper body is black (dark brown), and the belly and eye rings are white. The light-brown female is usually hornless. Blackbucks usually roam the plains in herds of 15 to 20 animals with on dominant male.

3. Diet

The diet of the Blackbuck consists mostly of grasses, although it does eat pods, flowers and fruits to supplement its diet. The maximum life span recorded is 16 years and the average is 12 years.

4. Threats

- Poaching
- Predation
- Habitat destruction
- Overgrazing
- Diseases
- Inbreeding
- Visitors

The Blackbuck is hunted for its flesh and its skin. Although Indian law strictly prohibits the hunting of these endangered animals, there are still occasional incidents of poaching. The remaining populations are under threat from inbreeding. The natural habitat of the Blackbuck is being encroached upon by man's need for arable land and grazing ground for domesticated cattle. Exposure to domesticated cattle also renders the Blackbuck exposed to bovine diseases.

Blackbuck was the most hunted wild animal all over India. Until India's independence, many princely states used to hunt this antelope and the other local Indian gazelle, the Chin Kara with specially trained pet Asiatic Cheetah. Their habitat of vast grasslands converted into farmlands due to human population explosion.

Gaur

Scientific classification

Kingdom	:	Animalia
Phylum	:	Chordata
Class	:	Mammalia
Order	:	Artiodactyla
Family	:	Bovidae
Subfamily	:	Antilopinae
Genus	:	Bos
Species	:	B. gaurus

Binomial name

Bos gaurus (H. Smith, 1827)

Vital Statistics

Range	:	South and South East Asia
Weight		
Male	:	1000 - 1500 Kg
Female	:	700 - 1000 Kg
Body Length	:	250 – 360 Cm
Tail Length	:	70 – 100 Cm
Shoulder Height	:	70 – 220 Cm
Sexual Maturity	:	2 – 3 year
Gestation Period	:	275 days
Young per birth	:	1, rarely 2
Diet	:	Grasses, shoots
Life Span	:	30 years

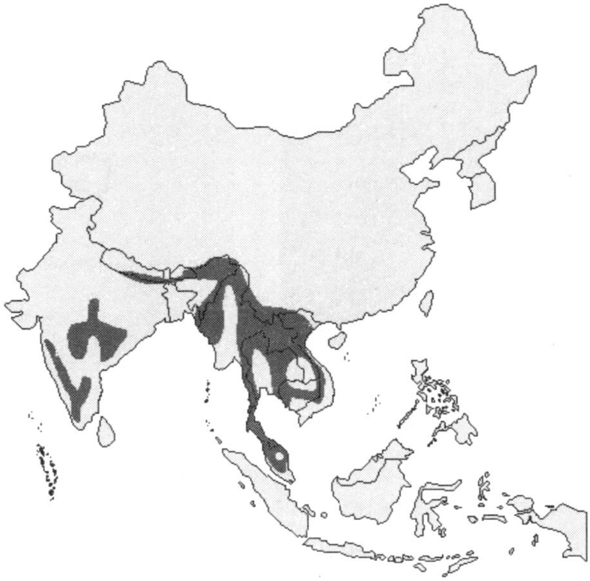

The Gaur (Bos gaurus, previously Bibos gauris) is a large, dark-coated ox of South Asia and Southeast Asia. The biggest populations are found today in India. It is also called seladang or in context with safari tourisms Indian bison, which is technically incorrect. The gaur is the largest of all wild cattle, bigger even than the Wild Asiatic Water Buffalo and Bison. The domesticated form of the gaur is called gayal or mithun.

1. Physical Characteristics

Gaur are said to look like the front of a water buffalo with the back of a domestic cow. They are the largest and most powerful of all wild cattle. Males have a highly muscular body, with a distinctive dorsal ridge and a large dewlap, forming a very powerful appearance. Females are substantially smaller, and their dorsal ridge and dewlaps are less developed. In colour the adult male gaur is dark brown, approaching black in very old individuals; the upper part of the head, from above the eyes to the nape of the neck, ashy gray, or occasionally dirty white; the muscle is pale coloured, and the lower part of the legs pure white. The cows and young bulls are paler, and in some instances have a rufous tinge, which is most marked in individuals inhabiting dry and open districts. The colour of the horns is some shade of pale green or yellow throughout the greater part of their length, but the tips are black.

2. Ecology and Behaviour

In the wild, gaurs live in small herds of up to 40 individuals and graze on grasses, shoots and fruits. Where gaurs have not been disturbed, they are basically diurnal, being most active in the morning and late afternoon and resting during the hottest time of the day. But where populations have been molested by human populations, gaurs have become largely nocturnal, rarely seen in the open after 8:00 in the morning. During the dry season, herds congregate and remain in small areas, dispersing into the hills with the arrival of the monsoon. While gaurs depend on water for drinking, they do not seem to bathe or wallow.

Due to their formidable size and power, the gaur has few natural enemies. Crocodiles, leopards, and dholes packs occasionally attack unguarded calves, but only the tiger has been reported to kill a full-grown adult. A family group consists of small mixed herds of 2-40 individuals. Gaur herds are led by an old adult female (the matriarch). Adult males may be solitary.

Himalayan Tahr

Scientific classification

Kingdom	:	Animalia
Phylum	:	Chordata
Class	:	Mammalia
Order	:	Artiodactyla
Family	:	Bovidae
Subfamily	:	Caprinae
Genus	:	Hemitragus
Species	:	H. jemlahicus

Binomial name

Hemitragus jemlahicus (H. Smith, 1826)

Vital Statistics

Range	:	India, Tibet
Weight	:	130 – 180 Kg
Length	:	120 - 170 Cm
Height	:	60 – 90 Cm
Gestation Period	:	7 Months
Young per birth	:	1
Diet	:	Grasses, shrubs
Life Span	:	18 years

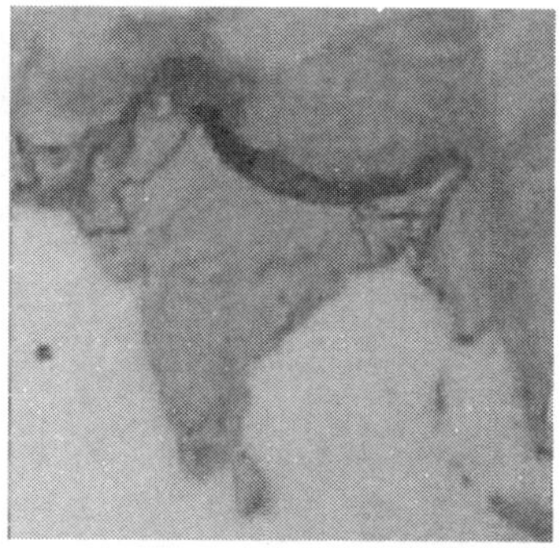

The Himalayan Tahr(Hemitragus jemlahicus) is a large ungulate and a close relative to the wild goat. Its native habitat is in the rugged wooded hills and mountain slopes of the Himalaya from northern India to Tibet. They spend the summers grazing in high pastures, then come down the mountains and from mixed-sex herds in the winter

1. Physical Characteristics

Himalayan Tahrs have relatively short legs and small heads with large eyes and small pointed ears. Their hooves have a flexible, rubbery core that allows them to grip smooth rocks, while a hard, sharp rim can lodge into small footholds. Males are larger and have different colouration and horn structure than the females. Adult Himalyan Tahrs range from 135 to 180 kg (300 to 400 lb) in weight, 120 to 170 cm in length, and 60 to 90 cm in height. They are herbivores, subsisting on grass, shrubs, and trees. The gestation period is seven months, and usually only one kid is born at a time. The young tahr nurses for about six months, and may follow its mother for up to two years. In the wild, tahrs can live up to 15 years, though ten years is more typical.

2. Conservation

The Himalayan Tahr is considered vulnerable by the World Conservation Union (IUCN) in its home range of the Himalaya.

Wild Yak

Scientific classification

Kingdom	:	Animalia
Phylum	:	Chordata
Class	:	Mammalia
Order	:	Artiodactyla
Family	:	Bovidae
Genus	:	Bos
Species	:	B. grunniens

Binomial name

Bos grunniens (Linnaeus, 1766)

Vital Statistics

Range	:	India
Weight	:	1200 Kg
Length	:	3250 mm
Sexual Maturity	:	6 – 8 Years
Breeding Season	:	September
Gestation Period	:	9.33 Months
Young per birth	:	1
Diet	:	Grasses, lichens
Life Span	:	6 - 8 years

The Yak is a long-haired bovine found throughout the Himalayan region. In addition to a large domestic population, there is a small, vulnerable wild yak population. Wild yaks (Tibetan: drong) can weigh up to 1,200 kg (2,400 lb). They usually form groups of between 10 and 30 animals. Their habitat is treeless uplands like hills, mountains and plateaus between 3,200 m (10,500 ft) and roughly 5,400 m (18,000 ft). They eat grasses, lichens and other plants. They are insulated by dense, close, matted under-hair as well as their shaggy outer hair. Yaks secrete a special sticky substance in their sweat which helps keep their under-hair matted and acts as extra insulation. This secretion is used in traditional Nepalese medicine. Many wild Yaks are killed for food by the Tibetans; they are now a vulnerable species.

Khajuria's Leaf-nosed Bat

Scientific classification

Kingdom	:	Animalia
Phylum	:	Chordata
Class	:	Mammalia
Order	:	Chiroptera
Family	:	Hipposideridae
Genus	:	Hipposideros
Species	:	H.durgadasi

Binomial name

Hipposideros durgadasi (Khajuria, 1970)

Vital Statistics

Tail	:	Enclosed in membrane
Ears	:	Large, no tragus
Muzzle	:	Complex noseleaf, no sella and lancet

The Khajuria's Leaf-nosed Bat(Hipposideros durgadasi) is species of bat in the Hipposideridae family. It is endemic to India. Its natural habitat is caves. It is threatened by habitat loss.

Kerala Rat

Scientific classification

Kingdom	:	Animalia
Phylum	:	Chordata
Class	:	Mammalia
Order	:	Rotentia
Family	:	Muridae
Genus	:	Rattus
Species	:	R.ranjiniae

Binomial name

Rattus ranjiniae (Arawal & Ghosal, 1969)

Vital Statistics

Common Name	:	Ranjinis rat
Occurrence	:	Endemic to Thiruvananthapuram District, Kerala
Identification	:	Can be distinguished by its large, pale hind feet and shorter palate
Diet	:	Seeds, grass
Social groups	:	2 – 3
Activity	:	Nocturnal
Stratum	:	Terrestrial, fossorial
Common threats	:	Pesticides, Human interference

The Kerala Rat (Rattus ranjiniae) is a species of rodent in the Muridae family. It is found only in India. Its natural habitats are subtropical or tropical dry lowland grassland and swamps.

Jackal

Scientific classification

Kingdom	:	Animalia
Phylum	:	Chordata
Class	:	Mammalia
Order	:	Carnivora
Family	:	Canidae
Genus	:	Canis
Species	:	Canis aureus

Binomial name

Canis aureus (Linnaeus, 1758)

Vital Statistics

Range	:	India
Weight	:	15 – 33pounds
Shoulder Size	:	15 – 20 inches
Gestation Period	:	About two months
Diet	:	Omnivorous, scavenger
Life Span	:	10 - 12 years

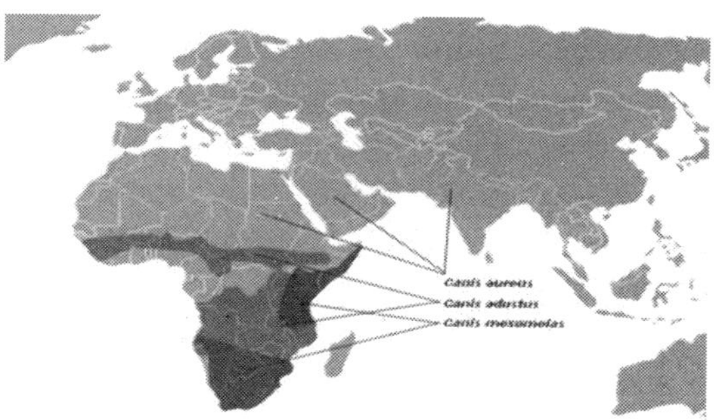

The **Golden Jackal** (*Canis aureus*), also called the **Asiatic, Oriental** or **Common Jackal** is a carnivorous mammal of the family Canidae native to north and east Africa, southeastern Europe and South Asia to Burma. It is the largest of the jackals.

Physical characteristics

The Golden Jackal's short, coarse fur is usually yellow to pale gold and brown-tipped, though the color can vary with season and region. The Golden Jackal is generally 70–105 centimetres (28–42 inches) in length, with a tail length of about 25 centimetres (10 in). Its standing height is approximately 38–50 cm (16–20 in) at the shoulder. Average weight is 7–15 kilograms (15–33 pounds) with males tending to be 15% heavier than the females.

Habitat

The common jackal lives in open savannas, deserts and arid grasslands. Side-striped jackals are found in moist savannas, marshes, bushlands and mountains. The sliver-backed jackal lives primarily in savannas and woodlands.

Diet

Jackals can best be described as opportunistic omnivores. They cooperatively hunt small or young antelopes and also eat reptiles, insects, ground-dwelling birds, fruits, berries and grass. They will pick over kills made by large carnivores and even frequent rubbish dumps in pursuit of food.

Predators and Threats

Being highly adaptable and resourceful, jackals have not displayed large population depletions like many other African carnivores. However, increased habitat loss causes them to infringe more and more on human settlements, where they may be viewed as a danger to livestock and poultry.

LEAST CONCERN

Red Fox

Scientific classification

Kingdom	:	Animalia
Phylum	:	Chordata
Class	:	Mammalia
Order	:	Carnivora
Family	:	Canidae
Genus	:	Vulpes
Species	:	**V.vulpes**

Binomial name

Vulpes vulpes (Linnaeus, 1758)

Vital Statistics

Range	:	Asia, Europe
Weight	:	2.7 – 6.8 Kg
Length	:	52.5 Cm
Height	:	67 Cm
Sexual Maturity		10 Months
Mating Season	:	December - January
Young per birth	:	5
Diet	:	Insects, molluses, earthworms and cray fish
Life Span	:	3 years

The **Red Fox** (Vulpes vulpes) is a mammal of the Carnivora. It has the widest range of any terrestrial carnivore, being native to Canada, Alaska, almost all of the contiguous United States, Europe, North

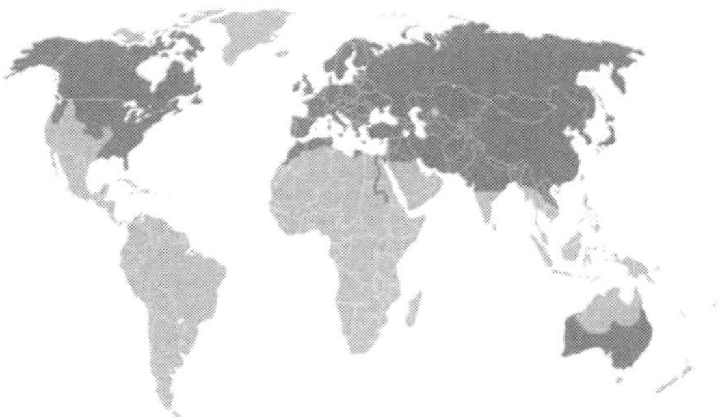

Africa and almost all of Asia, including Japan. As its name suggests, its fur is predominantly reddish-brown.

1. Distribution

Three subspecies of Red Fox are found in India: Vulpes vulpes Montana (the **Tibetan Fox**) found in Ladakh and the Himalayas, Vulpes vulpes griffithi(the **Kashmir Fox**) found in Jammu and Kashmir less the Ladakh sector, and Vulpes vulpes pusilla (the **Desert Fox**) found in the Thar Desert of Rajasthan and in Kutch, Gujarat.

2. Physical characteristics

The Red Fox has most commonly a rusty red, with white underbelly, black ear tips and legs, and a bushy tail with a distinctive white tip. The "red" tone can vary from crimson to golden, and in fact can be brindled or agouti, with bands of red , brown, black and white on each individual hair when seen close up.

The fox's eyes are gold to yellow and have distinctive vertically slit pupils, similar to those of a feline. Their eyesight is also as sharp as that of a feline, and combined with their extreme agility for a canid, the Red Fox has been referred to as "the cat-like canid". Its long bushy tail with distinctive white tip provides balance for large jumps and complex movement. It's strong legs allow it to reach speeds of over 70 km/h (45 miles per hour), a great benefit to catching prey or evading predators.

The Red Fox may reach an adult weight of 2.7-6.8 kg (6-15 lb), but this varies from region to region. During the autumn and winter, the Red Fox will grow more fur. This so-called "winter fur" keeps the animal warm in the colder environment. The fox sheds this fur at the onset of spring, reverting back to the short fur for the duration of the summer.

3. Ecology

The Red Fox is found in a variety of biomes, from prairies and scrubland to forest settings.

4. Dietary habits

Red Foxes are largely carnivorous. The majority of their diet consists of invertebrates, such as insects, mollusks, earth worms and crayfish. They do also eat some plant material, especially blackberries, apples, plums and other fruit. Common vertebrate prey includes rodents (such as mice and voles), rabbits, birds, eggs, amphibians, small reptiles and fish. Foxes have been known to kill deer fawns. They typically eat 0.5 to 1 kg (1-2 lb) of a food day. They usually hunt alone. With their acute sense of hearing, they can locate small mammals in thick grass, and they jump high in the air to pounce on the prey. They also stalk prey such as rabbits, keeping hidden until close enough to catch them in a short dash. Foxes tend to be extremely possessive of their food and will not share it with others.

5. Behaviour

The Red Fox displays a wide variety of behaviours. It is most active at night and at twilight. It is generally a solitary hunter. If a fox catches more food than it can eat, it will bury the extra food (cache) to store it for later. In general, each fox claims its own territory; it pairs up only in winter, foraging alone in the summer. The Red Fox has been considered a monogamous species, however evidence for polygamy (polygyny and polyandry) includes males' extra-territorial movements during breeding season (possibly searching for additional mates).

6. Threats

The Red Fox is of **some importance** in the fur industry. The fur of a silver fox was once considered by the natives of **New England** to be worth over 40 beaver skins. A chieftan accepting a gift of silver fox fur was seen as an act of reconciliation. Silver foxes were first commercially bred on Prince Edward Island, Canada in 1878. Red foxes are among the most commonly bred animals in fur farms, along with American Minks.Today , silver fox is traditionally used for collars and cuffs, wraps and stoles, while common red fox fur is used for trimming and for full fur garments.

Leopard

Scientific classification

Kingdom	:	Animalia
Phylum	:	Chordata
Class	:	Mammalia
Order	:	Carnivora
Family	:	Felidae
Genus	:	Panthera
Species	:	P.pardus

Binomial name

Panthera pardus (Linnaeus, 1758)

Vital Statistics

Range	:	India, Indonesia, Malaysia, China
Weight		
Male	:	37 – 90 Kg
Female	:	28 – 60 Kg
Length (Head & Body)	:	90 – 190 Cm
Tail Length	:	10 – 110 Cm
Shoulder Height	:	45 – 80 Cm
Mating Season	:	All year round
Gestation Period	:	90 - 105 days
Young per birth	:	2 – 3 cubs
Birth Interval	:	2 – 3 years
Diet	:	Monkeys, Antelopes
Life Span	:	10 - 15 years

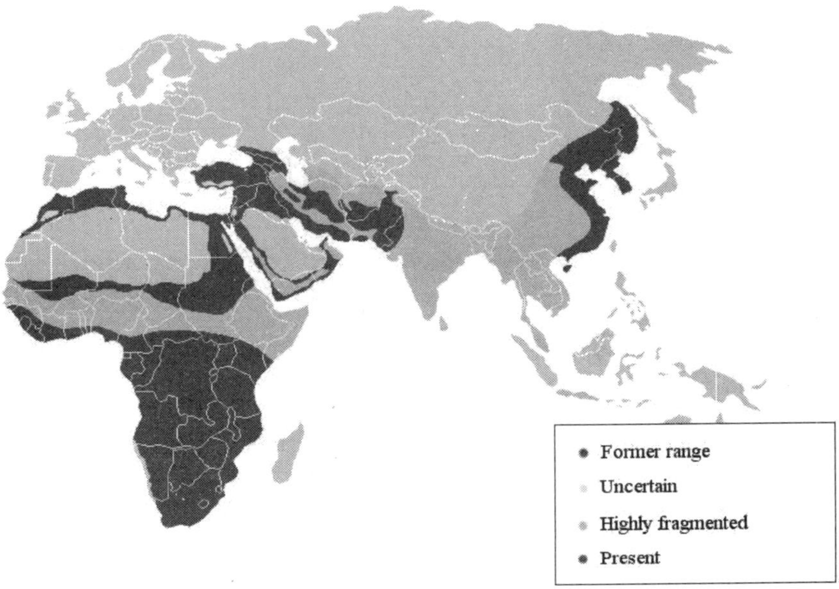

The Leopard is the fifth largest feline in the world behind the tiger, lion, jaguar and mountain lion. Leopards are strongly built and have a large head with extremely strong jaw muscles. They are graceful, stealthy animals and they are well known for their ability to go undetected. They are very agile climbers, good swimmers and probably the most accomplished stalker of all the big cats. Leopards have a light tan base coloured coat with a black rosette pattern and a lighter coloured underside.

1. Distribution

Leopards are the most widespread feline and they can be found in Africa, India, China, Korea and Siberia. They are very adaptable and live in open savannah, forests, jungles and mountainous areas. Leopards also like to live in grasslands, woodlands and riverside forests. They are solitary animals and males have territories between 5 and 40 sq. Kms (3 -25 sq. miles). They make the boundaries with urine and are very defensive of them. Their territory will overlap those of several females.

2. Physical characteristics

The leopard is an agile and graceful predator. Although smaller than the other members of Panthera, the leopard is still able to take large

pray given a massive skull that well utilizes powerful jaw muscles. Its is comparatively long for a cat and its legs are short. Head and body length is between 90 and 190 cm, the tail reaches 60 to 110cm. Shoulder height is 45 to 80cm. Males are considerably larger than females and weigh 37 to 91compared to 28 to 60 kg for females.

3. Ecology

As of 1996, the leopard had the largest distribution of any wild cat,[8], although populations before and since have shown a declining trend are fragmented outside of sub-Saharan Africa. The IUCN notes that within sub-Saharan Africa the species is "still numerous and even thriving in marginal habitats" where other large cats have disappeared, but that populations in North Africa may be extinct. In Asia, data on distribution are mixed: populations in Southwest and Central Asia are small and fragmented; in the northeast portion of the range, they are critically endangered; and in Indian, Southeast Asia, and China, the cat is still relatively abundant. Leopards also like to live in grasslands, woodlands and riverside forests.

4. Behaviour

Leopards are opportunistic hunters. The leopard stalks its prey silently and at the last minute pounces on its prey and strangles its throat with a quick bite. Leopards often hide their kills in dense vegetation or take them up trees, [13] , and are capable of carrying animals up to three times their own weight this way. The leopard is solitary and, aside from mating, interactions between individuals appear to be infrequent. Aggressive encounters have been observed.

National Parks of India

This is a list of all **national parks of India**. India's first national park (an IUCN category II protected area) was established in 1935 as *Hailey National Park*, now known as Jim Corbett National Park. By 1970, India only had five national parks. In 1972, India enacted the Wildlife Protection Act and Project Tiger to safeguard habitat; further federal legislation strengthening protections for wildlife was introduced in the 1980s. As of April 2007, there are 96 national parks. All national park lands encompass a combined 38,029.18 km², 1.16% of India's total surface area.

A total of 166 national parks have been authorized. Plans are underway to establish the remaining scheduled parks. All of India's national parks are listed below alongside their home state or territory and the date that they were established. For an overview of Indian protected areas in general, please see protected areas of India.

List of national parks

Name	State	Started	Area (in km²)
1. Anshi National Park	Karnataka	1987	250
2. Balphakram National Park	Meghalaya	1986	220
3. Bandhavgarh National Park	Madhya Pradesh	1982	448.85
4. Bandipur National Park	Karnataka	1974	874.20
5. Bannerghatta National Park	Karnataka	1974	104.27
6. Vansda National Park	Gujarat	1979	23.99
7. Betla National Park	Jharkhand	1986	231.67
8. Bhitarkanika National Park	Orissa	1988	145
9. Blackbuck National Park, Velavadar	Gujarat	1976	34.08
10. Buxa Tiger Reserve	West Bengal	1992	117.10
11. Campbell Bay National Park	Andaman and Nicobar	1992	426.23
12. Chandoli National Park	Maharashtra	2004	317.67
13. Corbett National Park	Uttarakhand	1936	520.82
14. Dachigam National Park	Jammu and Kashmir	1981	141
15. Desert National Park	Rajasthan	1980	3162
16. Dibru-Saikhowa National Park	Assam	1999	340

Name	State	Started	Area (in km²)
17. Dudhwa National Park	Uttar Pradesh	1977	490.29
18. Eravikulam National Park	Kerala	1978	97
19. Fossil National Park	Madhya Pradesh	1983	0.27
20. Galathea National Park	Andaman and Nicobar	1992	110
21. Gangotri National Park	Uttarakhand	1989	1552.73
22. Gir National Park	Gujarat	1975	258.71
23. Gorumara National Park	West Bengal	1994	79.45
24. Govind Pashu Vihar	Uttarakhand	1990	472.08
25. Great Himalayan National Park	Himachal Pradesh	1984	754.40
26. Gugamal National Park	Maharashtra	1987	361.28
27. Guindy National Park	Tamil Nadu	1976	2.82
28. Gulf of Kachchh Marine National Park	Gujarat	1980	162.89
29. Gulf of Mannar Marine National Park	Tamil Nadu	1980	6.23
30. Hemis National Park	Jammu and Kashmir	1981	4100
31. Hazaribag National Park	Jharkhand	N/A	183.89
32. Indira Gandhi National Park (prev: Annamalai National Park)	Tamil Nadu	1989	117.10
33. Indravati National Park	Chhattisgarh	1981	1258.37
34. Intanki National Park	Nagaland	1993	202.02
35. Kalesar National Park	Haryana	2003	100.88
36. Kanha National Park	Madhya Pradesh	1955	940
37. Kanger Ghati National Park (Kanger Valley)	Chhattisgarh	1982	200
38. Kasu Brahmananda Reddy National Park	Andhra Pradesh	1994	1.42
39. Kaziranga National Park	Assam	1974	471.71
40. Keibul Lamjao National Park	Manipur	1977	40
41. Keoladeo National Park	Rajasthan	1981	28.73
42. Khangchendzonga National Park	Sikkim	1977	1784
43. Kishtwar National Park	Jammu and Kashmir	1981	400
44. Kudremukh National Park	Karnataka	1987	600.32
45. Madhav National Park	Madhya Pradesh	1959	375.22

Name	State	Started	Area (in km²)
46. Mahatma Gandhi Marine National Park (prev: Wandur National Park)	Andaman and Nicobar	1983	281.50
47. Mahavir Harina Vanasthali National Park	Andhra Pradesh	1994	14.59
48. Manas National Park	Assam	1990	500
49. Mathikettan Shola National Park	Kerala	2003	12.82
50. Middle Button Island National Park	Andaman and Nicobar	1987	0.64
51. Mollem National Park	Goa	1978	107
52. Mouling National Park	Arunachal Pradesh	1986	483
53. Mount Abu Wildlife Sanctuary	Rajasthan	1960	288
54. Mount Harriet National Park	Andaman and Nicobar	1987	46.62
55. Mrugavani National Park	Andhra Pradesh	1994	3.60
56. Mudumalai National Park	Tamil Nadu	1990	103.24
57. Mukurthi National Park	Tamil Nadu	1990	78.46
58. Murlen National Park	Mizoram	1991	200
59. Nagarhole National Park	Karnataka	1988	643.39
60. Namdapha National Park	Arunachal Pradesh	1983	1985.23
61. Nameri National Park	Assam	1998	200
62. Nanda Devi National Park	Uttarakhand	1982	630.00
63. Navegaon National Park	Maharashtra	1975	133.88
64. Neora Valley National Park	West Bengal	1986	88
65. Nokrek National Park	Meghalaya	1986	47.48
66. North Button Island National Park	Andaman and Nicobar	1987	0.44
67. Orang National Park	Assam	1999	78.80
68. Palani Hills National Park	Tamil Nadu	Propose d	736.87
69. Panna National Park	Madhya Pradesh	1973	542.67
70. Pench National Park, Madhya Pradesh	Madhya Pradesh	1975	292.85
71. Pench National Park	Maharashtra	1975	257.26
72. Periyar National Park	Kerala	1982	350

Name	State	Started	Area (in km²)
73. Phawngpui Blue Mountain National Park	Mizoram	1997	50
74. Pin Valley National Park	Himachal Pradesh	1987	675
75. Rajaji National Park	Uttarakhand	1983	820.42
76. Rajiv Gandhi National Park	karnataka	2003	200
77. Rani Jhansi Marine National Park	Andaman and Nicobar	1996	256.14
78. Ranthambore National Park	Rajasthan	1980	392
79. Saddle Peak National Park	Andaman and Nicobar	1987	32.54
80. Salim Ali National Park	Jammu and Kashmir	1992	9.07
81. Sanjay National Park[2]	Chhattisgarh	1981	1471.13
82. Sanjay National Park[2]	Madhya Pradesh	1981	466.88
83. Sanjay Gandhi National Park a.k.a. Borivili National Park, Mumbai	Maharashtra	1983	86.96
84. Sariska National Park	Rajasthan	1982	273.80
85. Satpura National Park	Madhya Pradesh	1981	585.17
86. Silent Valley National Park	Kerala	1984	89.52
87. Sirohi National Park	Manipur	1982	0.41
88. Simlipal National Park	Orissa	1980	845.70
89. Singalila National Park	West Bengal	1992	78.60
90. South Button Island National Park	Andaman and Nicobar	1987	0.03
91. Sri Venkateswara National Park	Andhra Pradesh	1989	353.62
92. Sultanpur National Park	Haryana	1989	1.43
93. Sundarbans National Park	West Bengal	1984	1330.10
94. Tadoba National Park	Maharashtra	1955	116.55
95. Valley of Flowers National Park	Uttarakhand	1982	87.50
96. Valmiki National Park	Bihar	1989	335.65
97. Van Vihar National Park	Madhya Pradesh	1979	4.45

PLACES YOU CAN VISIT

On the Map Below are marked some of the best places to see wildlife in India. NP stands for National Park and WLS for Wildlife Sanctuary - the two categories of protected areas in India. Wildlife can also be seen outside the protected areas and these are indicated wherever appropraite.

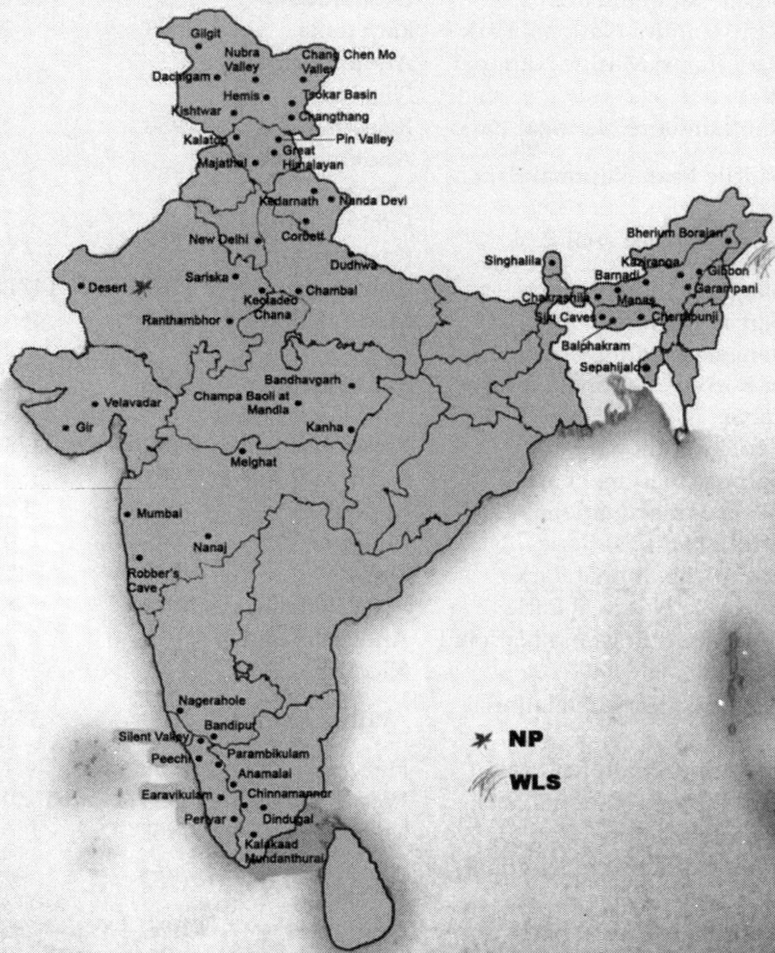

Wildlife Sanctuaries of India

India has over 500 animal sanctuaries, referred to as *Wildlife Sanctuaries* (IUCN Category IV Protected Area). Among these, the 28 Tiger Reserves are governed by Project Tiger, and are of special significance in the conservation of the tiger. Some wildlife sanctuaries are specifically named *Bird Sanctuary*, eg. Keoladeo National Park before attained National Park status. Many National Parks were initially Wildlife Sanctuaries.

Wildlife Sanctuaries

	Year	Name	State	Area (km^2)
1.	1979	Great Indian Bustard	Maharashtra	8496.44
2.	1986	Kutch Desert	Gujarat	7506.22
3.	1973	Wild Ass	Gujarat	4953.7
4.	ND	Nelapattu	Andhra Pradesh	4404
5.	1991	Dibang Valley	Arunachal Pradesh	4149
6.	1987	Changthang	Jammu & Kashmir	4000
7.	1978	Nagarjunasagar Srisailam	Andhra Pradesh	3568
8.	ND	Karakoram	Jammu & Kashmir	1800
9.	1978	Kaimur	Bihar	1342.22
10.	ND	Gundlabrahmeswaram	Andhra Pradesh	1194
11.	1965	Gir	Gujarat	1153.42
12.	1975	Noradehi	Madhya Pradesh	1034.52
13.	1972	Kedarnath	Uttar Pradesh	975.24
14.	1965	Kawal	Andhra Pradesh	893
15.	1952	Pakhal	Andhra Pradesh	879.3
16.	1977	Pakhui	Arunachal Pradesh	861.95
17.	1979	Simlipal	Orissa	845.7
18.	ND	Dandeli	Karnataka	834.16
19.	1953	Eturnagaram	Andhra Pradesh	803
20.	1987	Lachipora	Jammu & Kashmir	800
21.	1976	Satkosia Gorge	Orissa	795.52
22.	1989	Kamlang	Arunachal Pradesh	783
23.	1976	Palamau	Jharkhand	767
24.	1981	Narayan Sarovar (Chinkara)	Gujarat	765.79
25.	1976	Ratapani	Madhya Pradesh	688.79
26.	1976	Bhimbandh	Bihar	681.9
27.	1983	Keladevi	Rajasthan	676

	Year	Name	State	Area (km²)
28.	1963	Kolleru	Andhra Pradesh	673
29.	1977	Kinnerasani	Andhra Pradesh	655.41
30.	1962	Sechu Tuan Nala	Himachal Pradesh	655.32
31.	1979	National Chambal	Uttar Pradesh	635
32.	ND	Rollapadu	Andhra Pradesh	614
33.	1978	Tamor Pingla	Madhya Pradesh	608.52
34.	1982	Schoolpaneshwar	Gujarat	607.7
35.	1988	Sunabema	Orissa	600
36.	1986	Askot	Uttarakhand	599.93
36. A	1985	Melghat	Maharashtra	597.23
37.	1978	Papikonda	Andhra Pradesh	590.68
38.	1971	Kumbhalgarh	Rajasthan	578.26
39.	ND	Mundanthurai	Tamil Nadu	567.38
40.	1974	Sitanadi	Madhya Pradesh	553.36
41.	1975	Achanakmar	Madhya Pradesh	551.55
42.	1989	Balaram-Ambaji	Gujarat	542.08
43.	1987	Biligiri Rangswamy Temple	Karnataka	539.52
44.	1977	Bori	Madhya Pradesh	518.25
45.	1981	Ghatigaon	Madhya Pradesh	512
46.	1983	Phulwari	Rajasthan	511.41
47.	1987	Cauvery	Karnataka	510.51
48.	1986	Andhari	Maharashtra	509.27
49.	ND	Srivenkateshwara	Andhra Pradesh	506.94
50.	1982	Kaimoor	Uttar Pradesh	500.75
51.	1985	Dampa	Mizoram	500
52.	1976	Pulicat	Andhra Pradesh	500
53.	1983	Todgarh Raoli	Rajasthan	495.27
54.	1974	Bhadra	Karnataka	492.46
55.	ND	Srivilliputhur	Tamil Nadu	485.2
56.	1954	Govind Pashu Vihar	Uttar Pradesh	481.04
57.	1978	Bagdogra	Madhya Pradesh	478.9
58.	1950	Periyar	Kerala	472
59.	ND	Srilanka Malleswara	Andhra Pradesh	464.42
60.	1977	Pachmarhi	Madhya Pradesh	461.85
61.	1978	Valmikinagar	Bihar	461.6
62.	ND	Pulicat	Tamil Nadu	461.02
63.	1987	Sohagabarwa	Uttar Pradesh	428.2

	Year	Name	State	Area (km²)
64.	1987	Overa-Aru	Jammu & Kashmir	425
65.	1985	Koyna	Maharashtra	423.55
66.	1979	Sita Mata	Rajasthan	422.94
67.	1962	Tundah	Himachal Pradesh	419.48
68.	1974	Sharavathi Valley	Karnataka	413.23
69.	1976	Kateraniaghat	Uttar Pradesh	400.09
70.	1981	Kotgarh	Orissa	399.05
71.	1974	Shettihally	Karnataka	395.6
72.	1928	Manas	Assam	391
73.	1988	Gumti	Tripura	389.54
74.	1958	Radhangiri	Maharashtra	371.88
75.	1974	Gandhi Sagar	Madhya Pradesh	368.62
76.	1975	Sanjay (Dubri)	Madhya Pradesh	364.69
77.	1976	Singhalila	West Bengal	362.4
78.	1986	Kalsubai Harishchandra	Maharashtra	361.71
79.	ND	Kaundinya	Andhra Pradesh	357
80.	1982	Rupi Bhabha	Himachal Pradesh	354.14
81.	1983	Sardarpur Florican	Madhya Pradesh	348.12
82.	1985	Debrigarh	Orissa	346.91
83.	ND	Kuno - Palpur	Madhya Pradesh	345
84.	1981	Palpur - Kuno Wildlife Sanctuary	Madhya Pradesh	344.68
85.	1973	Waynad	Kerala	344.44
86.	1986	Jaikwadi	Maharashtra	341.05
87.	1978	Samarsot	Madhya Pradesh	340.35
88.	1962	Kugti	Himachal Pradesh	330
89.	1986	Painganga	Maharashtra	324.62
90.	1983	Pong Dam Sanctuary	Himachal Pradesh	322.7
91.	ND	Mudumalai	Tamil Nadu	321.55
92.	1978	National Chambal	Madhya Pradesh	320
93.	1985	Chandoli	Maharashtra	308.97
94.	1982	Ramgarh Bundi	Rajasthan	307
95.	1988	Badrama	Orissa	304.03
96.	1987	Sonanandi	Uttar Pradesh	301.18
97.	1982	Jamwa Ramgarh	Rajasthan	300
98.	1980	Marine (Gulf of Kutch)	Gujarat	293.03
99.	1960	Mountabu	Rajasthan	288.84
100.	1976	Singhori (Sindhari)	Madhya Pradesh	287.91
101.	1973	Parambikulam	Kerala	285

	Year	Name	State	Area (km²)
102.	1980	Mehao	Arunachal Pradesh	281.5
103.	1983	National Chambal	Rajasthan	280
104.	1972	Gomardah	Madhya Pradesh	277.82
105.	1984	Kuldiha	Orissa	272.75
106.	1955	Darah	Rajasthan	265.83
107.	1983	Pamed Wild Buffalo	Madhya Pradesh	262
108.	1986	Gautala Autramghat	Maharashtra	260.61
109.	1976	Gautam Buddha	Bihar	259.48
110.	1986	Buxa	West Bengal	251.89
111.	1988	Kanji	Jammu & Kashmir	250
112.	1983	Udanti Wild Buffalo	Madhya Pradesh	247.59
113.	1974	Mukambika	Karnataka	247
114.	1983	Panpatha	Madhya Pradesh	245.84
115.	1976	Barnawapra	Madhya Pradesh	244.66
116.	1962	Nargu	Himachal Pradesh	243.13
117.	1962	Bandli	Himachal Pradesh	239.47
118.	1978	Coringa	Andhra Pradesh	235.79
119.	1977	Ranipur	Uttar Pradesh	230.31
120.	1983	Bhensrodgarh	Rajasthan	229.14
121.	1972	Kishanpur	Uttar Pradesh	227.12
122.	ND	Kalakkadu	Tamil Nadu	223.58
123.	1989	Eaglenest	Arunachal Pradesh	217
124.	1990	Jaldapara	West Bengal	216.51
125.	1987	Spike Island	Andaman & Nicobar Islands	211.7
126.	1978	Lawalang	Bihar	211.03
127.	1985	Nakti Dam	Bihar	206.4
128.	1986	Kabar	Bihar	204
129.	1981	Karera	Madhya Pradesh	202.21
130.	1975	Intanki	Nagaland	202.02
131.	ND	Krishna	Andhra Pradesh	194.81
132.	1976	Dalma	Bihar	193.22
133.	1985	Baretha	Rajasthan	192.76
134.	1979	Barda	Gujarat	192.31
135.	1978	Hadgarh	Orissa	191.06
136.	1978	D'ering Memorial	Arunachal Pradesh	190
137.	1975	Abohar	Punjab	188.24
138.	1976	Hazaribagh	Bihar	186.25
139.	1987	Gulmarg	Jammu & Kashmir	186

	Year	Name	State	Area (km²)
140.	1985	Lakhari Valley	Orissa	185.87
141.	1989	Yagoupokpi Lokchao	Manipur	184.8
142.	1974	Bramhagiri	Karnataka	181.29
143.	1978	Jessore	Gujarat	180.66
144.	1985	Koderma	Bihar	177.95
145.	1969	Yawal	Maharashtra	177.52
146.	1982	Chandaka Dampara	Orissa	175.79
147.	1934	Sonai Rupai	Assam	175
148.	1987	Trishna	Tripura	170.56
149.	1981	Baisipalli	Orissa	168.35
150.	1990	Purna	Gujarat	160.84
151.	1970	Nagzira	Maharashtra	152.81
152.	1991	Ngengpui	Mizoram	150
153.	1967	Bhagwan Mahavir	Goa	148.52
154.	1992	Karlapat	Orissa	147.66
155.	1978	Itanagar	Arunachal Pradesh	140.3
156.	1983	Bhairamgarh	Madhya Pradesh	138.95
157.	1985	Nameri	Assam	137.07
158.	1980	Pranahita	Andhra Pradesh	136.02
159.	1986	Chaprala	Maharashtra	134.78
160.	1985	Interview Island	Andaman & Nicobar Islands	133
161.	1985	Bhimashankar	Maharashtra	130.78
162.	1990	Jambughoda	Gujarat	130.38
163.	1952	Pocharam	Andhra Pradesh	130
164.	1958	Neyyar	Kerala	128
165.	1976	Murti Wildlife	West Bengal	127.22
166.	1958	Peechi Vazhani	Kerala	125
167.	ND	Kheoni	Madhya Pradesh	122.7
168.	1969	Nal Sarovar	Gujarat	120.82
169.	1962	Gobind Sagar & Naina Devi	Himachal Pradesh	120.67
170.	1974	Ranebennur	Karnataka	119
171.	1982	Khalasuni	Orissa	116
172.	1987	Chautala	Haryana	113.96
173.	1983	Fensatallite	Madhya Pradesh	110.24
174.	1976	Chail	Himachal Pradesh	110.04
175.	1987	Hirpora	Jammu & Kashmir	110
176.	ND	Sundha Mata	Rajasthan	107

	Year	Name	State	Area (km²)
177.	1949	Gamgul Siahbehi	Himachal Pradesh	105.46
178.	1987	Talakaveri	Karnataka	105
179.	1984	Chimony	Kerala	105
180.	1968	Bhagwan Mahavir	Goa	105
181.	1975	Badankhoh	Madhya Pradesh	104.35
182.	1984	Sawai Mansingh	Rajasthan	103.25
183.	1987	Pushpagiri	Karnataka	102.59
184.	1984	Shenduruny	Kerala	100.32
185.	1986	Nandpur Madmeshwar	Maharashtra	100.12
186.	1989	Sessa Orchid	Arunachal Pradesh	100
187.	1980	Jawahar Sagar	Rajasthan	100
188.	1983	Shergarh	Rajasthan	98.71
189.	1962	Darlaghat	Himachal Pradesh	98.71
190.	1984	Chinnar	Kerala	90.44
191.	1974	Someswara	Karnataka	88.4
192.	1986	Aner Dam	Maharashtra	82.94
193.	ND	Mukkurthi	Tamil Nadu	78.46
194.	1957	Chandra Prabha	Uttar Pradesh	78
195.	1976	Idukki	Kerala	77
196.	1988	Katepurna	Maharashtra	73.69
197.	1985	Orang	Assam	72.6
198.	1984	Balukhand Konark	Orissa	71.72
199.	1962	Shikari Devi	Himachal Pradesh	71.19
200.	1979	Laokhowa	Assam	70.14
201.	1975	Bhitarkanika	Orissa	70
202.	1986	Phansad	Maharashtra	69.79
203.	1976	Tirthan	Himachal Pradesh	68.25
204.	1976	Mahuadaur	Bihar	63.25
205.	1954	Kanawar	Himachal Pradesh	61.57
206.	1970	Bor	Maharashtra	61.1
207.	1955	Van Vihar	Rajasthan	59.93
208.	1974	Narsingarh	Madhya Pradesh	57.19
209.	1985	Churdhar	Himachal Pradesh	56.59
210.	1982	Ratanmahal	Gujarat	55.65
211.	1991	Kane	Arunachal Pradesh	55
212.	1984	Aralam	Kerala	55
213.	1983	Peppara	Kerala	53
214.	1956	Jaisamand	Rajasthan	52
215.	1984	Barsey Rhododendron Sanctuary	Sikkim	51.76

	Year	Name	State	Area (km²)
216.	1984	Fambong Lho	Sikkim	51.76
217.	1980	Nahargarh	Rajasthan	50
218.	1974	Melkote Temple	Karnataka	49.82
219.	1984	Parasnath	Bihar	49.23
220.	ND	Pabha	Assam	49
221.	1988	Binsar	Uttarakhand	45.59
222.	1981	Ken Gharial	Madhya Pradesh	45
223.	1982	Harike Lake	Punjab	43
224.	1981	Sone Gharial	Madhya Pradesh	41.8
225.	1991	Khawnglung	Mizoram	41
226.	1989	Dipor Beel	Assam	40
227.	1989	Paniya	Gujarat	39.63
228.	1981	Surinsar-Mansar	Jammu & Kashmir	39.58
229.	1976	Senchal	West Bengal	38.88
230.	1987	Pobitora Wildlife Sanctuary	Assam	38.83
231.	1962	Raksham Chitkul	Himachal Pradesh	38.27
232.	1976	Lothian Island	West Bengal	38
233.	1962	Naina Devi	Himachal Pradesh	37.19
234.	1978	Siwaram	Andhra Pradesh	36.29
235.	1962	Talra	Himachal Pradesh	36.16
236.	1978	Rajgir	Bihar	35.84
237.	1987	Maenam	Sikkim	35.34
238.	1981	Nandini	Jammu & Kashmir	33.72
239.	1984	Shingba Rhododendron	Sikkim	32.5
240.	1987	Overa	Jammu & Kashmir	32.37
241.	1962	Majathal	Himachal Pradesh	31.64
242.	1954	Manali sanctuary	Himachal Pradesh	31.27
243.	1949	Kalatop & Khajjiar	Himachal Pradesh	30.69
244.	1970	Tansa	Maharashtra	30.41
245.	1974	Nugu	Karnataka	30.32
246.	1974	Ghataprabha	Karnataka	29.78
247.	1962	Lippa Asrang	Himachal Pradesh	29.53
248.	1987	Landfall Island	Andaman & Nicobar Islands	29.48
249.	1987	Malvan Marine	Maharashtra	29.12
250.	1981	Nongkhyllem	Meghalaya	29
251.	1962	Daranghati	Himachal Pradesh	27.01
252.	1980	Barnadi	Assam	26.22

	Year	Name	State	Area (km²)
253.	1987	Limber	Jammu & Kashmir	26
254.	[[]]	Sukhna	Chandigarh	25.42
255.	1983	Thattekkad Bird	Kerala	25
256.	1983	Crocodile (Lohabrrack)	Andaman & Nicobar Islands	22.21
257.	1986	Hastinapur	Uttar Pradesh	20.73
258.	ND	Tongri	Jammu & Kashmir	20
259.	1978	Manjira	Andhra Pradesh	20
260.	1987	Sepahijala	Tripura	18.53
261.	1954	Khokhan	Himachal Pradesh	17.6
262.	ND	Point Calimere	Tamil Nadu	17.26
263.	1958	Simbalbara	Himachal Pradesh	17.2
264.	1987	Chilka Lake (Nalaban)	Orissa	15.53
265.	1988	Rampura	Gujarat	15.01
266.	1985	Arabithittu	Karnataka	13.5
267.	ND	Indira Priyadarshini	Delhi	13.2
268.	1983	Sailana Florican	Madhya Pradesh	12.96
269.	1981	Ramnagar	Jammu & Kashmir	12.9
270.	1954	Kais	Himachal Pradesh	12.2
271.	1975	Bir Shikargarh	Haryana	10.93
272.	1985	Sagershwar	Maharashtra	10.87
273.	1987	Defence Island	Andaman & Nicobar Islands	10.49
274.	ND	Hokarsar	Jammu & Kashmir	10
275.	1987	Cinque Island	Andaman & Nicobar Islands	9.51
276.	1987	Flat Island	Andaman & Nicobar Islands	9.36
277.	1987	Buchaan Island	Andaman & Nicobar Islands	9.33
278.	1977	Barren Island	Andaman & Nicobar Islands	8.1
279.	1987	Kyd Island	Andaman & Nicobar Islands	8
280.	1972	Bondla Wildlife	Goa	8
281.	1987	Shearme Island	Andaman & Nicobar Islands	7.85
282.	1987	Paget Island	Andaman & Nicobar Islands	7.36
283.	1985	Tilanchang Island	Andaman & Nicobar Islands	6.83
284.	1977	Narcondum Island	Andaman & Nicobar Islands	6.81
285.	1987	West Island	Andaman & Nicobar Islands	6.4
286.	1987	East Island	Andaman & Nicobar Islands	6.11
287.	1976	Halliday Island	West Bengal	5.95
288.	1987	Ranger Island	Andaman & Nicobar Islands	4.26
289.	1987	Swamp Island	Andaman & Nicobar Islands	4.09
290.	1987	East (Inglis) Island	Andaman & Nicobar Islands	3.55
291.	1977	North Reef Island	Andaman & Nicobar Islands	3.48

	Year	Name	State	Area (km²)
292.	1987	Benett Island	Andaman & Nicobar Islands	3.46
293.	1987	Talabaicha Island	Andaman & Nicobar Islands	3.21
294.	1987	Point Island	Andaman & Nicobar Islands	3.07
295.	1987	Baltal	Jammu & Kashmir	3
296.	1987	Bondoville Island	Andaman & Nicobar Islands	2.55
297.	1987	Table (Delgarno) Island	Andaman & Nicobar Islands	2.29
298.	1985	Battimalve Island	Andaman & Nicobar Islands	2.23
299.	1987	James Island	Andaman & Nicobar Islands	2.1
300.	1979	Dr. Salim Ali Bird Sanctuary	Goa	1.8
301.	1987	Reef Island	Andaman & Nicobar Islands	1.74
302.	1987	Table (Excelsior) Island	Andaman & Nicobar Islands	1.69
303.	1977	South Sentinel Island	Andaman & Nicobar Islands	1.61
304.	1987	Sandy Island	Andaman & Nicobar Islands	1.58
305.	1987	Roper Island	Andaman & Nicobar Islands	1.46
306.	1987	Pitman Island	Andaman & Nicobar Islands	1.37
307.	1987	South Brother Island	Andaman & Nicobar Islands	1.24
308.	1987	South Reef Island	Andaman & Nicobar Islands	1.17
309.	1987	Bluff Island	Andaman & Nicobar Islands	1.14
310.	1987	Sir Huge Rose Island	Andaman & Nicobar Islands	1.06
311.	1987	Temple Island	Andaman & Nicobar Islands	1.04
312.	1987	Ross Island	Andaman & Nicobar Islands	1.01
313.	ND	Ranganthittu	Karnataka	0.67
314.	ND	Bir Motibagh	Punjab	ND
315.	ND	Bhagmara	Meghalaya	ND
316.	ND	Tal Chappar	Rajasthan	ND
317.	ND	Renuka	Himachal Pradesh	ND
318.	ND	Shilli	Himachal Pradesh	ND
319.	ND	Bir Bunnerheri	Punjab	ND
320.	ND	Bassi	Rajasthan	ND
321.	ND	National Garhial	Rajasthan	ND
322.	ND	Khijadiya	Gujarat	ND
323.	ND	Bir Gurdialpura	Punjab	ND
324.	ND	Asan Bradge Bird Watching	Uttar Pradesh	ND
325.	ND	Chilla	Uttar Pradesh	ND
326.	ND	Mahavir Swamy	Uttar Pradesh	ND
327.	ND	Nawabganj	Uttar Pradesh	ND
328.	ND	Samaspur	Uttar Pradesh	ND

	Year	Name	State	Area (km^2)
329.	ND	Dhakna Kolkaz	Maharashtra	ND
330.	ND	Gandhari	Maharashtra	ND
331.	ND	Wainganga	Maharashtra	ND
332.	ND	Dhumkhal	Gujarat	ND
333.	ND	Ushakothi	Orissa	ND
334.	ND	Chandra Prabha	Bihar	ND
335.	ND	Topchanchi	Bihar	ND
336.	ND	Bibnutibhushan	West Bengal	ND
337.	ND	Betuadahary	West Bengal	ND
338.	ND	Ballavpur	West Bengal	ND
339.	ND	Chapramari	West Bengal	ND
340.	ND	Gorumara	West Bengal	ND
341.	ND	Jorpokhri	West Bengal	ND
342.	ND	Mahananda	West Bengal	ND
343.	ND	Parnadhan	West Bengal	ND
344.	ND	Ramnabagan	West Bengal	ND
345.	ND	Raiganj	West Bengal	ND
346.	ND	Kyongasia Alpine	Sikkim	ND
347.	ND	Garampani	Assam	ND
348.	ND	Siju	Meghalaya	ND
349.	ND	Pulebatze	Nagaland	ND
350.	ND	Fakim	Nagaland	ND
351.	ND	Charilam	Tripura	ND
352.	ND	Lanjamadugu	Andhra Pradesh	ND
353.	ND	Karikili	Tamil Nadu	ND
354.	ND	Vedantangal	Tamil Nadu	ND
355.	ND	Vettangudi	Tamil Nadu	ND
356.	ND	Vallanadu	Tamil Nadu	16.41
357.	ND	Kumarakom	Kerala	ND

* ND- No Details

References

- **Oliver, William L. R. (1980).** The Pigmy Hog: the Biology and Conservation of the Pigmy Hog, Sus (Porcula) salvanius, and the Hispid Hare, Caprolagus hispidus. Special Scientific Report No 1. Jersey Wildlife Preservation Trust.
- **Narayan, Goutam (2006).** Pygmy Hog Conservation Programme – an update. Suiform Soundings, PPHSG Newsletter, Volume 6, Pages 14-15.
- **Funk, Stephan M., Sunil Kumar Verma, Greger Larson, Kasturi Prasad, Lalji Singh, Goutam Narayan and John E. Fa (2007).** The pygmy hog is a unique genus: 19th century taxonomists got it right first time round. Molecular Phylogenetics and Evolution, Volume 45, Pages 427-436.
- **Walston, J. and P.J.J Bates. 2001**. The discovery of Wroughton's free-tailed bat Otomops wroughtoni (Chiroptera: Molossidae) in Cambodia. Acta Chiropterologica, 3(2): 249-252.
- **Shivaji,S. , D. Jayaprakash and Suresh B. Patil (1998)** Assessment of inbreeding depression in big cats: Testosterone levels and semen analysis. Current science. 75(9):23-30 [1].
- **Ravi Chellam and A.J.T. Johnsingh (1999),** Translocating Asiatic Lions, India RE-INTRODUCTION NEWS No. 18, Page 11.
- **Macdonald, David (1984).** *The Encyclopedia of Mammals: 1*, pp.446. ISBN 0-04-500028-x.
- **Brown, Gary (1996).** *Great Bear Almanac*, pp.340. ISBN 1558214747.
- **Islav Mazak: Der Tiger. Nachdruck der 3. Auflage von 1983. Westarp Wissenschaften Hohenwarsleben, 2004** ISBN 3 894327596.
- **Dinerstein, Eric (2003),** *The Return of the Unicorns; The Natural History and Conservation of the Greater One-Horned Rhinoceros*, New York: Columbia University Press, ISBN 0-231-08450-1.
- **Hoffmann, Robert S.; Andrew T. Smith (2005-11-16).** in Wilson, D. E., and Reeder, D. M. (eds): *Mammal Species of the World*, 3rd edition, Johns Hopkins University Press, 194-195. ISBN 0-801-88221-4.
- **Groves, C. (2005-11-16)**. in Wilson, D. E., and Reeder, D. M. (eds): *Mammal Species of the World*, 3rd edition, Johns Hopkins University Press, 178-179. ISBN 0-801-88221-4.
- **Mootnick, A.; Groves, C. P. (2005).** "A new generic name for the hoolock gibbon (Hylobatidae)". *International Journal of* ^ Groves, C.

(2005-11-16). in Wilson, D. E., and Reeder, D. M. (eds): *Mammal Species of the World*, 3rd edition, Johns Hopkins University Press, 164. ISBN 0-801-88221-4.

- **Singh Mewa and Kaumanns Werner (2005-10-10).** "Behavioural studies: A necessity for wildlife management". *Current Science* **89** (7): 1233.
- **Ramachandran, K. K.; Joseph, Gigi, K. (2001).** "*Distribution and demography of diurnal primates in Silent Valley National Park and adjacent areas, Kerala, India*". *Journal of the Bombay Natural History Society* **98** (2): 191–196.
- **Singh Mewa and Kaumanns Werner (2004-10).** "Distribution and Abundance of Primates in Rain Forests of the Western Ghats, Karnataka, India and the Conservation of Macaca silenus". *International Journal of Primatology* **25** (5): abstract. doi:10.1023/B:IJOP.0000043348.06255.7f.
- **Wozencraft, W. C. (16 November 2005).** in Wilson, D. E., and Reeder, D. M. (eds): *Mammal Species of the World*, 3rd edition, Johns Hopkins University Press. ISBN 0-801-88221-4.
- **Srivastava, A.; J. Biswas & J. Das et al. (2001),** "Status and Distribution of Golden Langurs (*Trachypithecus geei*) in Assam, India", *American Journal of Primatology* **55** (1): 15-23, DOI 10.1002/ajp.1035.
- **Gee, E. P. (1961).** The distribution and feeding habit of golden langur, *Presbytis geei* (Khajuria, 1956). J. Bombay Nat. His. Soc. 53: 252–254.
- **Rekha Medhi, Dilip Chetry, P. C. Bhattacharjee and B. N. Patiri (2004)** Status of *Trachypithecus geei* in a Rubber Plantation in Western Assam, India. International Journal of Primatology 25(6):1331-1337.
- **Musser, G. G. and M. D. Carleton. 2005.** Superfamily Muroidea. Pp. 894-1531 *in* Mammal Species of the World a Taxonomic and Geographic Reference. D. E. Wilson and D. M. Reeder eds. Johns Hopkins University Press, Baltimore.
- **Gardner, Alfred (November 16, 2005).** in Wilson, D. E., and Reeder, D. M. (eds): *Mammal Species of the World*, 3rd edition, Johns Hopkins University Press, 107. ISBN 0-801-88221-4.
- **Nowak, Ronald M. (1999).** *Walker's Mammals of the World*. Johns Hopkins University Press. ISBN 0-8018-5789-9.
- **Snow Leopard Fact Sheet".** ***Snow Leopard Trust*** **(2008).** Retrieved on 2008-10-23.
- **"Snow Leopard profile".** ***National Geographic*** **(2008).** Retrieved on 2008-10-23.

- **"Population and Protections"**. ***Snow Leopard Trust*** **(2008)**. Retrieved on 2008-07-03.
- **Snow Leopard Conservancy. 2006**. *Training park managers in the conservation of snow leopards.* Retrieved 27 November 2006.
- **Wade, Matt (February 15, 2008),** "Threat to a national symbol as India's wild tigers vanish", *The Age (Melbourne)*: 9.
- **Karanth, K.U., Nichols, J.D., Seidensticker, J., Dinerstein, E., Smith, J.L.D., McDougal, C., Johnsingh, A.J.T., Chundawat, R.S. (2003)** Science deficiency in conservation practice: the monitoring of tiger populations in India. Animal Conservation (61): 141-146 Full text.
- **Schaller. G *The Deer and the Tiger: A Study of Wildlife in India* 1984,** University Of Chicago Press.
- **Karanth, K. Ullas; Sunquist, Melvin E. (2000).** "Behavioural correlates of predation by tiger (*Panthera tigris*), leopard (*Panthera pardus*) and dhole (*Cuon alpinus*) in Nagarahole, India". *Journal of Zoology* 250: 255–265.
- **Datta, Aparajita & S. P. Goyal (1996),** "Comparison of Forest Structure and Use by the Indian Giant Squirrel (*Ratufa indica*) in Two Riverine Forests of Central India", *Biotropica* 28 (3): 394-399.
- **Moore, Joseph Curtis (1960),** "Squirrel Geography of the Indian Subregion", *Systematic Zoology* 9 (1): 1-17.
- **Prater, S. H. (1971),** *The book of Indian Animals,* Mumbai: Bombay Natural History Society and Oxford University Press. Pp. *xxiii*, 324, 28 colour plates by Paul Barruel., ISBN 0195621697.
- **Somanathan, Hema; Subhash Mali & Renee M. Borges (2007),** "Arboreal larder-hoarding in tropical Indian giant squirrel *Ratufa indica*", *Ecoscience* 14 (2): 165-169,
- **Tritsch, Mark F. (2001),** *Wildlife of India,* London: Harper Collins Publishers. Pp. 192, ISBN 0007110626.
- **Musser, G. G. and M. D. Carleton. 2005**. Superfamily Muroidea. Pp. 894-1531 *in* Mammal Species of the World a Taxonomic and Geographic Reference. D. E. Wilson and D. M. Reeder eds. Johns Hopkins University Press, Baltimore.
- **Bunnell, Fred (1984)**. in Macdonald, D.: *The Encyclopedia of Mammals*. New York: Facts on File, 96. ISBN 0-87196-871-1.
- **"Natural History of the Red Fox"**. *Wildlife Online*. Retrieved on **2007-09-09**.
- **Kothari, Ashok S. & Chhapgar, Boman F. (eds). 2005**. *The Treasures of Indian Wildlife*. Bombay Natural History Society and Oxford University Press, Mumbai.

- **Vivek menon, (2003)** A field guide to Indian mammals, Dorling Kindersley (India) Pvt. Limited and Penguin Book India (p) Ltd ISBN 0 - 14 - 302998 - 3; pp. 201.

Websites

1. www.webindia123.com
2. www.wildlifeofindia.com
3. www.travelmasti.com
4. www.indianwildlife.com
5. www.wii.gov.in
6. www.wikipedia.org
7. www.animalinfo.org
8. www.iucnredlist.org
9. www.wild-india.com
10. http://earthtrends.wri.org
11. www.indiawildlifetour.com

Index